Walden x 40

Walden x 40

ESSAYS ON THOREAU

ROBERT B. RAY

INDIANA UNIVERSITY PRESS
Bloomington and Indianapolis

This book is a publication of

Indiana University Press
601 North Morton Street
Bloomington, Indiana 47404-3797 USA

www.iupress.indiana.edu

Telephone orders   800-842-6796
Fax orders   812-855-7931

⊚ The paper used in this publication
meets the minimum requirements of
the American National Standard for
Information Sciences—Permanence
of Paper for Printed Library Materials,
ANSI Z39.48-1992.

Manufactured in the United States of
America

LIBRARY OF CONGRESS CATALOG-
ING-IN-PUBLICATION DATA

Ray, Robert B. (Robert Beverley), date.
 Walden x 40 : essays on Thoreau /
Robert B. Ray
  p. cm.
 Includes bibliographical references and
index.
 ISBN 978-0-253-35686-4 (cloth : alk.
paper) — ISBN 978-0-253-22354-8 (pbk.
: alk. paper)
 1. Thoreau, Henry David, 1817-1862.
Walden. 2. Thoreau, Henry David,
1817-1862—Homes and haunts—Massachusetts—Walden Woods. 3. Walden
Woods (Mass.). I. Title.
PS3048.R39   2011
818'.303—dc22   2011021189

1 2 3 4 5 17 16 15 14 13 12

TO HELEN, MARGARET, AND ELEANOR

To be a philosopher is not merely to have subtle thoughts, nor even to found a school. . . . It is to solve some of the problems of life, not only theoretically, but practically.

—Thoreau, *Walden*

I have at all times written my works with my whole body and my whole life; I don't know any purely "intellectual problems."

—Nietzsche

CONTENTS

ACKNOWLEDGMENTS

I want to thank Daniel Herwitz for his generous, insightful comments on the manuscript of this book. I am also grateful to Jane Behnken at Indiana University Press for her invaluable support and advice and to MJ Devaney for copyediting both rigorous and astute. Although Victor Perkins and Andrew Klevan are film scholars rather than Thoreauvians, their writings about the movies have informed this book in many ways. My thanks to Cary Crane, whose cover design provides a visual equivalent of *Walden*'s austere loveliness. Finally, my gratitude goes to James Naremore, Gregory Ulmer, and Christian Keathley for their continuing friendship and inspiration.

BIBLIOGRAPHICAL NOTE

All parenthetical page references to *Walden* cite *Walden, Civil Disobedience, and Other Writings*, 3rd ed., ed. William Rossi (New York: Norton, 2008).

Week refers to *A Week on the Concord and Merrimack Rivers*, ed. Carl F. Hovde, William L. Howarth, and Elizabeth Hall Witherell (Princeton: Princeton University Press, 1980).

J refers to Thoreau's *Journal*, which I have cited by date. I have used the fourteen-volume edition, *The Journal of Henry David Thoreau*, ed. Bradford Torrey and Francis H. Allen (Salt Lake City, UT: Peregrine Smith, 1984).

We now have at least two superb annotated editions of *Walden:*

Walden: An Annotated Edition, notes by Walter Harding (Boston: Houghton Mifflin, 1995).

Walden: A Fully Annotated Edition, ed. Jeffrey S. Cramer (New Haven: Yale University Press, 2004).

Walden x 40

INTRODUCTION

1.

In a 1991 survey, American academics named *Walden* "the single most important work to teach in nineteenth-century literature courses." Unlike most classics (including runners-up *The Scarlet Letter* and *Moby Dick*), Thoreau's book continues to find readers outside the classroom. Civil rights activists, environmentalists, stubborn misfits all have regularly turned to *Walden* for tactics or counsel, and as long as there are *Wandervogeln,* it will find a home. New editions—illustrated, annotated, excerpted for calendars or daybooks—appear annually. And yet almost everything that passes for common knowledge about Henry David Thoreau turns out to be wrong.

- First comes the matter of his name, which rhymes not with *hello* but with *thorough,* a homonym of which he would often take punning advantage. Christened David Henry Thoreau, he simply reversed the order of his first two names at some point after college, perhaps to acknowledge that his friends and parents had always called him Henry.
- Like Emerson, Thoreau went to Harvard, having grown up in Concord, a suburb of Boston; but his world was much smaller than those names now make it seem. Concord was a village of barely two thousand people, and Thoreau's Harvard class had fewer than fifty students, and the college itself only thirty-five faculty members.
- Thoreau didn't spend a few months in the woods, but over two years: twenty-six months, to be exact, from 4 July 1845 to 6 September 1847. He started work on his cabin (built on land

owned by Emerson) in March 1845, when Herman Melville was returning from his whaling voyage. He spent a week in 1845 at his parents' house while he winterized his cabin, and in 1846, he went on a two-week excursion to Maine.

• Although Thoreau writes about his decision to go to Walden in the most positive way ("I went to the woods because I wished to live deliberately" [65]), the move was also motivated by a vocational crisis: he had failed as a teacher, writer, and lecturer, and he didn't like working in his father's pencil factory, where he had achieved his one success by designing the lead pencil still in use today.

• Despite the popular image of his seclusion, Walden Pond was not remote, and Thoreau was not that solitary. The pond was only a mile and a half from Concord's center (less than a twenty-minute walk), and Thoreau not only had frequent visitors (including his mother and sister, who brought him home-cooked meals); he also went into town almost every day. As one biographer describes the situation, citing a contemporary, "Thoreau 'really lived at home, where he went every day', while he 'bivouacked' at his cabin." On one trip into Concord, he got jailed for refusing to pay his poll tax, an experience which resulted in the famous essay now known as "Civil Disobedience."

• Thoreau didn't finish *Walden* in the woods, although he appears to have written about half of it there. He did, however, write another book, *A Week on the Concord and Merrimack Rivers,* which he intended as a memorial to his brother with whom he had made that trip.

• *Walden* did not appear immediately after Thoreau's experiment; it was published seven years later, after seven drafts, while he struggled with occasional melancholy and the persisting issue of how to earn a living. The *Week*'s near-complete commercial failure contributed greatly to this delay.

• Although *Walden*'s small first edition eventually sold out, the book did not make Thoreau immediately famous. Indeed, for most of the nineteenth century, he was regarded as merely Emerson's protégé. The Thoreau revival occurred in the twentieth century, around the issues of political protest and environmentalism.

• Thoreau is usually grouped with the transcendentalists, whose philosophy, articulated by Emerson, amounted to a Neoplatonism, a faith that the world offers a set of signs or hieroglyphs to be deciphered for their truths—eternal, holy, and not of this earth. While Thoreau may have entered the woods as a transcendentalist, intent on "trying to hear what was in the wind" (15), he almost certainly emerged as something else, insisting that "We should be blessed if we lived in the present always" (211). His goal became not to read *through* the world but to immerse himself in it. In effect, he anticipated a comment by the twentieth-century philosopher Ludwig Wittgenstein:

> I might say: if the place I want to get to could only be reached by a ladder, I would give up trying to get there. For the place I really have to get to is a place I must already be at now. Anything that I might reach by climbing a ladder does not interest me.

• Thoreau's goal is to show himself, and us, a way out of the "lives of quiet desperation" (8) in which so many people have trapped themselves. Robert Richardson, one of Thoreau's best biographers, has encouraged us to "read this book. . . . It will make your life better." *Walden*'s therapy, however, requires a reorientation much harder than it seems. Again, one of Wittgenstein's remarks suggests the problem:

> It is as if a man is standing in a room facing a wall on which are painted a number of dummy doors. Wanting to get out, he fumblingly tries to open them, vainly trying them all, one after the other, over and over again. But of course it is quite useless. And all the time, although he doesn't realize it, there is a real door in the wall behind his back, and all he has to do is turn round and open it. To help him get out of the room all we have to do is to get him to look in a different direction. But it's hard to do this, since, wanting to get out he resists our attempts to turn him away from where he thinks the exit must be.

Thoreau insists that we can find the door leading to a joyful life only when we have learned to call things by their right names. Money, for example, is not just something we use to buy other commodities; it is a commodity itself, which has to be purchased.

"The cost of a thing," Thoreau proposes, "is the amount of what I will call life which is required to be exchanged for it, immediately or in the long run" (24).

• For all of *Walden*'s capacity to inspire, Thoreau himself can prove a stumbling block. A sympathetic reader, will often find passages so close to his own thoughts or concerns that he will feel that Thoreau could be his twin. But in other places, Thoreau can appear so repellant, so hectoring, so downright cranky that this same reader will want nothing to do with him. Emerson's eulogy addressed this problem, describing how difficult Thoreau could be, how demanding of his friends, how critical of anything short of perfection. By his example, he was forever telling them what he had already told himself: you must change your life.

2.

Despite *Walden*'s now well-established popular success, first-time readers are often surprised by its difficulty. Thoreau himself issued a warning about what his work would demand:

> To read well, that is, to read true books in a true spirit, is a noble exercise, and one that will task the reader more than any exercise which the customs of the day esteem. It requires a training such as the athletes underwent, the steady intention almost of the whole life to this object. Books must be read as deliberately and reservedly as they were written. (72)

This is a daunting proposition, one that not every reader will prove willing to accept. Part of the problem lies with *Walden*'s capacity to put off even its admirers. As Ronald B. Schwartz once admitted, in one of the best short essays on Thoreau, the book "often bores me when I'm near it, and enchants me all the rest of the time." How can we account for this effect? Does the fault lie with Thoreau or with ourselves? Even Thoreau said of his daily life at the pond, to which *Walden* devotes so much attention, "An old-fashioned man would have lost his senses or died of ennui" (90). How can we *train* ourselves to read this book?

We might start to answer this question by remembering two things. First, Thoreau described his trip to the woods as an "experiment" (31,

41, 47, 60), one of his favorite terms. Second, in writing *Walden,* Thoreau used the modular process he relied on for all of his extended works, shuffling and combining and revising journal entries triggered by his daily experiences over a period of years. He settled on this method early; by the summer of 1845, when he had taken up residence at Walden, he could describe it exactly:

> From all points of the compass from the earth beneath and the heavens above have come these inspirations and been entered duly in such order as they came in the Journal. Thereafter when the time arrived they were winnowed into lectures, and again, in due time, from lectures into essays. (*J,* summer 1845)

Although Thoreau struggled mightily to stitch his discrete entries into longer forms, he occasionally expressed regret, even while assembling *Walden,* at having done so:

> I do not know but thoughts written down thus in a journal might be printed in the same form with greater advantage—than if the related ones were brought together into separate essays. They are now allied to life—& are seen by the reader not to be far-fetched. It is more simple—less artful. . . .
> . . . Perhaps I can never find so good a setting for my thoughts as I shall thus have taken them out of. (*J,* 27 and 28 January 1852)

Thus, if we want to train ourselves to read *Walden,* perhaps we should take Thoreau at his word by adopting an experimental method that relies on fragments left as fragments, undiminished by a deferral of sustained exposition: this way of working might approach what Thoreau himself sought, something "more simple, less artful." After all, as *Walden* observes, "so little has been tried" (10).

This book presents the results of a training exercise designed to encourage a "deliberate" reading of *Walden,* specifically a writing assignment I set for my students and myself:

> Produce a paper consisting of at least twenty-six discrete essays, one for each letter of the alphabet, prompted by words or passages from *Walden.* Note the following suggestions:

1. This method works best when you begin with something from *Walden* that intrigues you without your being immediately able to say why. The initial mystery will provoke what Roland Barthes called "an interrogative reading." If you begin instead with an idea about Thoreau or *Walden* and cast around for something to hang it on, you will often find yourself rehearsing something you already knew rather than learning something you did not. In other words, use the writing process the way Thoreau used his sojourn in the woods—as a means of research and discovery.

2. Remember the rule of communication science: information is a function of surprise. If you find yourself repeatedly coming up with things that everybody knows, look around for other prompts, ones that at first you may not fully understand. A Thoreau *Journal* entry offers good advice: "I begin to see . . . objects only when I leave off understanding them" (J, 14 February 1851). While we want to further our understanding of *Walden,* we may need to start by simply being *puzzled* by it, using that initial mystification as our means.

At the very least, this exercise demands close reading: you cannot address the assignment without paying close attention to what Thoreau wrote. I was surprised, however, by the difficulty the task presented to even the best students. Or perhaps I should say, to *especially* the best students, for it is they who have become the virtuosos of deductive "readings," in which a theoretical concept, increasingly derived from the social sciences, gets applied to a literary text. My honors undergraduates would have much preferred writing a Marxist analysis of Thoreau's "Economy," or a gender study of his implicit sexuality, or a critique of his attitude toward Native Americans— they already knew how to produce such papers on demand, and they probably knew their conclusions in advance. Very few of them, however, had learned the art of "reading deliberately." But my students were smart and willing, and I hope this book demonstrates their qualities. Almost every one of its entries began with something one of them noticed about *Walden.* I have revised, expanded, and conflated their ideas, adding what I have come up with on my own. But I could not have written this book without the starting points they provided.

Some readers will remember that in a previous book, *The ABCs of Classic Hollywood*, I argued that this method responds to filmmaking, whose final product is an assemblage of discontinuous, individual shots. I am not retracting that proposition, but I am also suggesting that if Thoreau's compositional method, with its reliance on *Journal* passages written at different times and different places, does not anticipate the cinema, it at least works the same way. In Joseph Wood Krutch's description, Thoreau's approach to writing closely resembles the process of film editing:

> The moment of sustained and incisive illumination never existed, . . . the Orphic profundities. . . . had been written down as fragments, neither successive nor connected, and they were then, sometimes years later, carefully selected and carefully fitted together in such a way that what looks like explosive brilliance was actually the result of a patient craftsmanship carefully matching and arranging brilliants which had been hoarded one by one over the years.

Although Ludwig Wittgenstein appears prominently in what follows, my students and I have not produced a Wittgensteinian reading of *Walden*. Wittgenstein himself was eager to achieve "that understanding which consists in 'seeing connections,'" and I have traced *Walden*'s connections to a range of figures, including Wordsworth, Nietzsche, Breton, Sartre, and André Bazin. Nevertheless, the connections between Thoreau and Wittgenstein are especially numerous. Small and wiry; intensely self-absorbed; handy with tools and practical jobs; given to long walks, remote excursions, and daily writing—the two men were cut from the same cloth. Above all, both were preoccupied with the question of how to live, and both realized that only method would enable them to formulate an answer.

Nietzsche wrote of *Daybreak*, his own discontinuous work, that "a book such as this is not for reading straight through . . . but for dipping into . . . ; you must be able to stick your head into it and out of it again and again." This advice may apply to *Walden X 40*; certainly the book does not require one to read it "straight through." A reader who does so will almost certainly notice the recurrence of certain passages, cited and discussed in more than one essay. Ideally, these

Walden passages should take on a different aspect in each entry, like a city's landmark revealed from various approaches. Wittgenstein, in fact, offered that simile to explain his proposition that "the only way to do philosophy is to do everything twice": "In teaching you philosophy," he remarked, "I'm like a guide showing you how to find your way round London. . . . After I have taken you many journeys through the city, in all sorts of directions, we shall have passed through any given street a number of times—each time traversing the street as part of a different journey."

Thoreau is, above all, a *centripetal* writer. Everything he touches returns to the one question that concerns him: *how can I discover the best way to live my life? Walden* represents his attempt to devise a method for answering that question, and the key to that method is repetition. By staying at Walden for over two years, Thoreau made sure that he would do everything at least twice. In fact, the book demonstrates how the most ordinary things in our lives—a medium-sized pond, a path worn through the woods, the animals who share our domain, the night sky, our home town, a few friends—have an infinite number of aspects, forever renewing themselves with the change of seasons, in different times of day, in response to the permanent inconstancy of our own fluctuating moods. That lesson is the key to *Walden,* and learning it demands that we abandon impatience. We must be willing to return again and again to certain passages, hoping that each new encounter, arrived at by a different route, will produce what Thoreau celebrates—the capacity to find joy in the repetitions that constitute so much of our lives.

1.

ADVENTURE

When he has obtained those things which are necessary to life, there is another alternative than to obtain the superfluities; and that is, to adventure on life. (14)

Is *Walden* the record of an *adventure*? If so, why does Thoreau avoid using that word to describe his twenty-six months in the woods? Although *Walden* now stands as one of the great adventures in nineteenth-century American history, Thoreau clearly preferred to cast his project in scientific terms (see "Experiment"), perhaps hoping that a more clinical vocabulary would convince his neighbors that what might have looked like irresponsible idling was, in fact, rigorous research. He may also have sensed that the pond's proximity to Concord, and his own near-daily trips to town, would have made any claims of "adventure" seem ridiculous hyperbole: after all, to many of his townsmen, Thoreau was just camping out on Emerson's land, like a child in his parents' backyard.

But the issue is more complex. Thoreau himself loved travel books, especially those about explorers. And yet he dismisses this taste as a guilty pleasure: "I read one or two shallow books of travel in the intervals of my work," he confesses in *Walden*, "till that employment made me ashamed of myself, and I asked where it was then that *I* lived" (71). Thoreau will begin *Walden*'s "Conclusion" with an elaboration on this theme, converting it into an explicit exhortation:

Be rather the Mungo Park, the Lewis and Clarke and Frobisher of your own streams and oceans; explore your own higher latitudes.

... [B]e a Columbus to whole new continents and worlds within you, opening new channels, not of trade, but of thought. . . . Explore thyself. Herein are demanded the eye and the nerve. Only the defeated and deserters go to the wars, cowards that run away and enlist. (215–16)

For Thoreau, however, his own command proved difficult to obey, and the problem almost certainly involved his vexed attitude toward writing. For a start, how he could portray his Walden sojourn as "an adventure" when his neighbors must have quickly realized that he spent most of time there not exploring or hunting but writing? Thoreau himself seemed ambivalent about this activity, admitting in the *Week*, composed at Walden, that "it is not easy to write in a journal what interests us at any time, because to write it is not what interests us" (*Week*, 332).

Thoreau's career—and, indeed, his life—would turn on his ability to overcome this opposition. *Walden* amounts to the first demonstration, to himself as well as his readers, that writing does not foreclose the possibility of adventure but rather enables it. In effect, Thoreau anticipated the lesson of Sartre's Antoine Roquentin (in *Nausea*):

For the most banal event to become an adventure, you must (and this is enough) begin to recount it. . . . Nothing happens while you live. The scenery changes, people come in and go out, that's all. There are no beginnings. Days are tacked on to days without rhyme or reason, an interminable, monotonous addition. . . .

That's living. But everything changes when you tell about life.

It's tempting to think that such telling amounts to casting a spell, an enchantment that will endow the world around us, and our very selves, with a newfound splendor. In Thoreau's hands, however, writing prompted a kind of attention that requires becoming clear eyed. Only by looking at the world with a vision stripped of habit and custom can we begin to take on the role that Nietzsche would announce "as adventurers and circumnavigators of that inner world which is called 'human being', as surveyors." In the years following his stay at Walden, Thoreau, of course, would make his primary living as a surveyor, but he also continued to write in his journal almost every day. He would teach himself that writing made even the most ordinary day, with all of its eventlessness and unexceptional weather, an adventure.

2.

ANTS

In the celebrated, mock-heroic rendering of an ant war, from "Brute Neighbors," appears the source of Walden's difficulty, its alternation between inspiration and tedium. For like all virtuosic set pieces, in which rhetorical brilliance remains thematically undermotivated, this passage serves primarily as a record of *the desire to write*. As such, it implies underemployment, a modern condition detectable in places like the *Village Voice*, where grandly educated, poorly paid intellectuals huff and puff over the latest pop records. With Thoreau, this twin condition of being out of work and eager to write finds its confirmation in his journal's twenty-six volumes, a labor impossible for a working man.

Thoreau's desire to write, however, confronted him with immediate problems. For a major prose writer, he has the least gift for narrative imaginable; even the anecdote eludes him. Thus, going to Walden appealed to him because there *nothing could happen*. Even Thoreau's situation, a mere mile and a quarter from his family's house, deprived his book of *Robinson Crusoe*'s great propelling question: will the hero get home? Thoreau, in effect, was *already* home, so *Walden* had to take up other things. Dismissive of both official news and local gossip, Thoreau effectively isolated himself from *information*, the sine qua non of storytelling. As a result, *Walden* had to redefine information, insisting on Nature's communiqués.

Even more important, having abandoned narrative, it had to rely on the other two organizing modes, exposition/argument and the poetic. *Walden*, of course, still offers the bare outline of a tale: searching for life and how to live it, a man abandons society for a solitary sojourn in the woods. Thoreau, however, minimizes this narrative's momentum, consistently using its elements for exhortation ("Simplify, simplify") or lyricism. The ant passage suggests the problem. Serving as a substitute for anything that would normally register as a narrative *event,* the War of the Ants demands Thoreau's compensating expository and poetic skills, thereby providing a model of *Walden's* challenge: namely, how, in the absence of narrative, to keep the reader's interest. The book's intermittent failures find their best explanation in the work of the 1920s French impressionist filmmakers. Refusing storytelling ("The telephone rings, and all is lost," Jean Epstein complained about a scene that launched a plot) and insisting on isolated moments of *photogénie,* this group proposed a cinematic practice that would strive for continuous visual poetry. That their movies now seem almost unrelievedly tedious suggests that in prose and filmmaking, by convention narrative mediums, the poetic registers most powerfully as *an interruption* of story, not as a substitute for it.

3.

AWAKE

Morning is when I am awake and there is a dawn in me. Moral
reform is the effort to throw off sleep. . . . To be awake is to be
alive. I have never yet met a man who was quite awake. How could
I have looked him in the face?

We must learn to reawaken and keep ourselves awake, not by
mechanical aids, but by an infinite expectation of the dawn. (64)

Walden's rich mysteriousness often derives from Thoreau's own
ambivalence. "The fact is," he reported to his journal, "I am a mystic,
a transcendentalist, and a natural philosopher to boot" (*J*, 5 March
1853). Emerson's Neoplatonic transcendentalism had regarded the
material world as a set of signs pointing to more important spiritual
truths, and *Walden* often reflects that lesson. Thus, although Thoreau provides the exact details of planting and nurturing his crops,
insisting "I was determined to know beans," he immediately shifts
registers: "Not that I wanted beans to eat . . . but, perchance, as some
must work in fields if only for the sake of tropes and expression, to
serve a parable-maker one day" (111). In "Brute Neighbors," a chapter
nominally devoted to the pond's wildlife, Thoreau strikes the same
note, proposing that "animals . . . are all beasts of burden, in a sense,
made to carry some portion of our thoughts" (153).

And yet Thoreau can also slam the door on a metaphysical flight
with sentences as matter-of-fact as Hemingway's. In a superb essay
on *Walden*, Stephen Fender calls attention to the passage in "Economy" where Thoreau describes how he had watched a striped snake

lying "without inconvenience" on the pond's bottom for over a quarter of an hour, "perhaps because he had not yet fairly come out of the torpid state." This observation prompts a miniature sermon:

> It appeared to me that for a like reason men remain in their present low and primitive condition; but if they should feel the influence of the spring of springs arousing them, they would of necessity rise to a higher and more ethereal life. (31–32)

This sentence is the Emersonian Thoreau. What follows is not:

> I had previously seen the snakes in frosty mornings in my path with portions of their bodies still numb and inflexible, waiting for the sun to thaw them. On the 1st of April it rained and melted the ice, and in the early part of the day, which was very foggy, I heard a stray goose groping about over the pond and cackling as if lost, or like the spirit of the fog. (32)

"It is hard to explain what makes this passage quite so appealing," Fender comments, suggesting that its effect depends on "the argument's willingness to wander." The oscillation between symbol and fact, both the longing for and the resistance to easy "correspondences," the commitment to saying what the woods were really like as well as what they might stand for—all lie at the heart of *Walden,* and a phrase like "on the first of April it rained and melted the ice" confirms Thoreau's proposition that "mere facts and names and dates communicate more than we suspect" (*J,* 27 January 1852). The pond repeatedly serves as a symbol, of course, but Thoreau also needs to tells us that in 1845, it "froze entirely over for the first time on the night of the 22d of December . . . ; in '46, the 16th; in '49, about the 31st; and in '50, about the 27th of December; in '52, the 5th of January; in '53, the 31st of December" (168). After celebrating nature's intimations of immortality and "the tonic of wildness," *Walden's* penultimate chapter, "Spring," ends with something like a ship captain's logbook entry: "Thus was my first year's life in the woods completed, and the second year was similar to it. I finally left Walden September 6th, 1847" (213–14).

Whatever the reason for Thoreau's divided attitude (his Oedipal struggle with Emerson? the influence of romanticism? a discomfort with ready-made pieties? his love of nature for its own sake? the ebb-ing of his imaginative powers?), *Walden's* appeal depends on it. If Emerson's determined commitment to "higher laws" has made his writing recede from us, nineteenth-century naturalists' straightfor-ward descriptions don't work either. It's the shuttling back and forth between fact and symbol that makes *Walden:* the pond becomes more than just a body of water, but we are more likely to accept it as an image of "the infinite" because we also know that in 1845, it "froze entirely over for the first time on the night of the 22nd of December."

In *Walden,* this relationship between the transcendental and the empirical involves less a simple alternation than a constant readjust-ment, as if Thoreau were dialing a knob to mix sounds coming from two different but related frequencies. The same tactic appears at the level of style, particularly in Thoreau's cunning deployment of cru-cial words in both their metaphorical and literal senses. Thus, the moralizing tone of the passage that heads this entry obviously pro-poses *wakefulness* as a metaphor for moral, intellectual, and spiritual awareness, with slumber standing for something like "the unexam-ined life" or even moral delinquency. "Why is it that men give so poor an account of their day," Thoreau asks, "if they have not been slumbering?"

They are not such poor calculators. If they had not been overcome with drowsiness they would have performed something. The mil-lions are awake enough for physical labor, but only one in a mil-lion is awake enough for effective intellectual exertion, only one in a hundred millions to a poetic or divine life. (64)

This figurative sense returns in *Walden's* "Conclusion," especially in its stirring last three sentences:

Only that day dawns to which we are awake. There is more day to dawn. The sun is but a morning star. (224)

In these contexts, therefore, Thoreau uses *awake* to mean something like what we would have in mind when addressing someone doing something absolutely wrongheaded: "Wake up!"

Earlier in the "Conclusion," however, the notion of wakefulness, or rather its opposite, slides towards the literal. "We know not where we are," Thoreau writes. "Beside, we are sound asleep nearly half our time." And, of course, except for insomniacs, we are. But Thoreau's own problem was insomnia's opposite, an inherited narcolepsy that *Walden* acknowledges with a joke:

> That winter . . . I labored with a lethargy,—which, by the way, I never knew whether to regard as a family complaint, having an uncle who goes to sleep shaving himself, . . . or as the consequence of my attempt to read Chalmers' collection of English poetry without skipping. (174)

Thus, a literal condition prompts Thoreau's predilection for a figurative usage.

Even that usage, however, is unstable. What does Thoreau mean by *wakefulness*? Alertness? Attentiveness? A state of heightened receptivity? In *The Prelude*, Wordsworth suggests what Thoreau was after: "There's not a man/That lives who hath not known his god-like hours" (3.193–94), when "a flash . . . has revealed/The invisible world" (6.601–602). Wordsworth identified this kind of wakefulness with "spots of time," privileged moments of "renovating virtue" (12.208, 210). To Thoreau, the obvious question presented itself; could one devise *a method* for achieving this state? In the light of this problem, *Walden* appears as an instruction manual designed to solve its author's own imperative: "We must learn to reawaken and keep ourselves awake." The diet, the clothes, the cabin, the solitude, the walks, even the idleness are all part of the formula in a book in which the desire for method, and the fear of its inadequacy, haunt everything. After leaving Walden, Thoreau began to feel this problem even more acutely. Although Robert Richardson mentions "Thoreau's nearly limitless capacity for being interested" as one of his greatest virtues, by 1851, four years after leaving the pond, he was already lamenting a failing inspiration: "I fear," he confided to his journal, "that the character of my knowledge is from year to year becoming more distinct & scientific—that, in exchange for views as wide as heaven's cope, I am being narrowed down to the field of the microscope" (J, 19 August 1851). But even this often cited passage does not tell the whole story without its rarely quoted conclusion, so characteristic of Thoreau's habitual movement between speculation and description, resembling the register shifts in *Walden's* frozen-snake passage:

> I see details, not wholes nor the shadow of the hole. I count some parts, and say, "I know." The cricket's chirp now fills the air in dry fields near pine woods. (*J*, 19 August 1851)

In one sense, Thoreau was only experiencing the typical romantic's fear of aging, directly expressed by Wordsworth:

> The days gone by
> Return upon me almost from the dawn
> Of life; the hiding places of man's power
> Open; I would approach them, but they close.
> I see by glimpses now; when age comes on,
> May scarcely see at all.
> (*The Prelude*, 10.277–82)

But there was another issue. *Walden* often suggests that Thoreau's desired wakefulness results less from deliberate effort than from sheer *chance,* a word that, along with its synonyms, appears with some frequency in *Walden:*

> Once it *chanced* that I stood in the very abutment of a rainbow's arch. (138)

> I am on the alert for the first signs of spring, to hear the *chance* note of some arriving bird. (203)

> We should be blessed if we lived in the present always, and took advantage of every *accident* that befell us, like the grass which confesses the influence of the slightest dew that falls on it. (211)

An 1841 journal entry admits to the writing's origins in something other than mere effort: "It is always a chance scrawl, and commemorates some accident" (8 February 1841). Not surprisingly, *Walden's* structure depends on its opening two chapters' strenuous purposefulness giving way to what Wordsworth called "a wise passiveness" as Thoreau settles down at the pond, and the book settles down to descriptions. While "Economy," "Where I Lived and What I Lived For," and the "Conclusion" advocate effort and determination, *Walden*'s overall tone is different—quieter, more contemplative, more reliant on what the wind might deliver each new day. This kind of wakefulness more closely resembles what Wallace Stevens describes in "Notes toward a Supreme Fiction":

> not balances
> That we achieve but balances that happen,
>
> As a man and woman meet and love forthwith.
> Perhaps there are moments of awakening,
> Extreme, fortuitous, personal, in which
>
> We more than awaken, sit on the edge of sleep,
> As on an elevation, and behold
> The academies like structures in a mist.

"On the edge of sleep," wakefulness's apparent antonym, accurately describes some of Thoreau's most privileged moments:

> Sometimes, in a summer morning, having taken my accustomed bath, I sat in my sunny doorway from sunrise till noon, rapt in a revery, amidst the pines and hickories and sumachs, in undisturbed solitude and stillness, while the birds sang around or flitted noiseless through the house, until by the sun falling in at my west window, or the noise of some traveller's wagon on the distant highway, I was reminded of the lapse of time. I grew in these seasons like corn in the night. (79)

Or a night's drowsy fishing-by-moonlight: "These experiences were very memorable and valuable to me" (120). *Walden*, in fact, recognizes the threshold between sleep and wakefulness as a site of revelation:

Every man has to learn the points of compass again as often as he awakes, whether from sleep or any abstraction. Not till we are lost, in other words, not till we have lost the world, do we begin to find ourselves, and realize where we are and the infinite extent of our relations. (118)

Anticipating Freud, Thoreau even suggests that sleep enables the appearance of the most urgent philosophical questions. "After a still winter night I awoke with the impression that some question had been put to me, which I had been endeavoring in vain to answer in my sleep, as what—how—when—where?" (189). Thoreau rises to these questions, but for all of his celebration of wakefulness, effort, deliberation, and "conscious endeavor," *Walden*'s most sublime moments often result from a submission to reverie, chance, and drowsy daydream.

(with Brenda Maxey-Billings,
Robert McDonald, and Adam Nikolaidis)

B

4.

BASKETS

Early in "Economy," Thoreau spins an anecdote into a parable:

Not long since, a strolling Indian went to sell baskets at the house of a well-known lawyer in my neighborhood. "Do you wish to buy any baskets?" he asked. "No, we do not want any," was the reply. "What!" exclaimed the Indian, as he went out the gate, "do you mean to starve us?" Having seen his industrious white neighbors so well off,—that the lawyer only had to weave arguments, and by some magic wealth and standing followed,—he had said to himself, I will go into business; I will weave baskets; it is a thing which I can do. Thinking that when he had made the baskets he would have done his part, and then it would be the white man's to buy them. He had not discovered that it was necessary for him to make it worth the other's while to buy them, or at least make him think that it was so, or to make something else which it would be worth his while to buy. I too had woven a kind of basket of a delicate texture, but I had not made it worth any one's while to buy them. Yet not the less, in my case, did I think it worth my while to weave them, and instead of studying how to make it worth men's while to buy my baskets, I studied rather how to avoid the necessity of selling them. (16)

The basket that Thoreau could not sell, of course, was his first book, *A Week on the Concord and Merrimack Rivers,* whose publication he had been forced to underwrite and which, as one critic observes, was "a commercial disaster, one of the worst-selling books by an eventual-ly-canonized author in American literary history." The book's failure plunged Thoreau into debt; he had to take back the unsold copies, thereby prompting his wry comment, "I have now a library of nearly nine hundred volumes, over seven hundred of which I wrote myself" (*J,* 27 October 1853). William E. Cain draws the conclusion Thoreau himself had reached: "He would not make a living from literature."

In fact, Thoreau was one of the first artists to encounter a pecu-liarly modern problem. Any writer, painter, or musician working in a new style would now have to assume that between the introduction of innovative work and its acceptance by the public a *gap* would inev-itably exist. An artist wanting a paying career would have to reduce it. This situation first appeared most prominently in France. In the wake of the French Revolution, the demise of the stable patronage system, which had rested on a small, sophisticated coterie, ready to commission and purchase art, resulted in an entirely new audience for painting—the bourgeoisie, newly come to power (both politically and financially) but less sophisticated, less secure about its own taste. Such an audience (the prototype of the generalist lost in a world of specialization) inevitably proved conservative, lagging behind the increasingly rapid stylistic innovations stimulated in part by this very system (which, after all, became a marketplace, thriving on nov-elty). Mass taste, in other words, now had to be educated to accept what it did not already know. Some artists simply looked for other ways to support themselves. Stendhal, who worked primarily as a quasi diplomat, resigned himself to not matching Balzac's commer-cial success: "I've bought a ticket in a lottery," he boasted, "the grand prize of which amounts to this: being read in 1935." He was right, of course, but unless an innovative artist remained content with post-humous success (represented as the only "genuine" kind by Balzac's *Lost Illusions,* a principal source of the avant-garde myth), he would need to develop strategies to eliminate the gap that would otherwise starve him.

In many ways, the French impressionist painters were the first avant-garde movement to think collectively and systematically about this dilemma. Some of them were working class and without other sources of income. When their work began to be rejected by the annual salons, virtually the only avenue to commercial success, they set in motion what retrospectively appear as "The Eight Rules for Starting an Avant-Garde."

1. *Collaboration.* Outsiders working together have a better chance of imposing themselves than does someone operating alone. The romantics (Coleridge and Wordsworth, Goethe and Schiller) had already taught this lesson; the impressionists understood it. As early as 1864, Monet, Renoir, Sisley, and Bazille were painting together in the forest of the Fontainebleau, and subsequently they shared Parisian studios or apartments. Even Manet, a relative loner, maintained an informal salon at the Café Guerbois, where writers (especially Zola) and other artists (like the photographer Nadar) mixed with the painters.

2. *The importance of the name.* A crucial factor in the impressionists' success was the movement's name, which Harrison and Cynthia White point out "was in the great tradition of rebel names. Thrown at them initially as a gibe to provide a convenient handle to insult them, it was adopted by the group in defiance and for want of a better term and made into a winning pennant." "Impressionism," in fact, aptly described much of their work; the name was easy to remember and carried with it the theoretical justification for a style that seemed unfinished, especially when compared to the *fini* or "licked" surface of the official, accepted contemporaries, the "Pompiers." No avant-garde group has ever achieved major acceptance without a catchy name: futurism, surrealism, fauvism, the new wave, even dada, a parody of such names. The name provides a group identity, offering a hook for critics and dealers, furthering publicity.

3. *The star.* Avant-garde movements need a key figure whose glamour and prolificness will attract the attention of outsiders. Cubism had Picasso, surrealism had Breton. The impressionists had Manet—rich, witty, articulate, and shocking while also being, by virtue of his training and disposition, the most clearly linked to the great tradition of French painting.

4. *Traditional training.* Even if an artist rejects its precepts, some encounter with a profession's more or less official schools will give him a sense of what to expect in the art world. With that work behind him, he will have a better chance of justifying his

own deviations by demonstrating that he has *chosen* to ignore standards others have mastered. In the twentieth century, nothing would help Picasso's reputation more than his masterful skills in conventional drawing. Almost all of the impressionists (Cézanne was the great exception) had studied at either the École des Beaux-Arts or privately with academic painters.

5. *The concept of the career.* The impressionists demonstrated the effectiveness of refocusing one's attention away from individual paintings to a whole career and its evolution. They understood that thinking in terms of a career meant constructing a narrative that would make sense of an artist's development.

6. *New avenues for distribution and exhibition.* With the Salon closed to them, the impressionists relied on their own alternatives: the Salons des Réfusés, group shows staged by dealers, and even one-man exhibitions. Durand-Ruel, the principal impressionist dealer, opened new markets for art, especially in America, by redefining art as an investment, a speculation with possibilities of appreciation, thereby enabling sales to the bourgeoisie, which understood money more than painting.

7. *Reconceptualization of the division of labor.* In the French academy system, painters (at least those enthroned in the Institut) also functioned as judges, selecting the works that appeared in the annual salons. They both painted and set the standards for new painting. Rapidly detecting this conflict of interest, which discouraged the reception of even slightly different work, the impressionists, perhaps imitating the burgeoning industrial revolution, divided the labor: painters stuck to painting, leaving to dealers and critics the task of assessment. In many ways, the avant-garde's history represents a constant tinkering with the division of labor, usually in ways that challenge existing arrangements. Duchamp chose to act not only as an artist but also as his own dealer and critic, thereby recombining the roles the impressionists had separated.

8. *The role of theory and publicity.* In *The Painted Word,* Tom Wolfe decried abstract expressionism's reliance on the criticism that sustained it. That symbiotic relationship, however, had begun much earlier. In 1815, Wordsworth had announced the new dispensation: "Every author, as far as he is great and at the same time *original,* has had the task of *creating* the taste by which he is to be

enjoyed." New styles, in other words, would henceforth demand *a new critical idea.* Impressionism encouraged a shift from arguments about subject matter to ones about style, benefiting both from Baudelaire's praise of "the painter of modern life" and the concept of "the impression," terms that legitimized their everyday, nonclassical subjects and the sketchy, unfinished appearance of so many of their paintings. Even more important, writers favorable to the impressionists redefined the notion of the artist, who became less an artisan, working for traditional patrons, than a romantic outsider, speculating on future recognition. This new critical idea turned conventional standards upside down. By recasting the academy as a group of outdated stuffed shirts, vestiges of the ancien régime's hostility to bourgeois economic and social power, the impressionists effectively identified the artist with his new client and made rejection by the academy *itself the sign of worth.* No one had thought of that idea before.

Thoreau, in fact, had many of these strategies available to him. He belonged to a group that had both a name (transcendentalism) and a star (Emerson). If that name's suggestion of abstract philosophy and quasi spiritualism often obscured the movement's practical ambitions and religious unorthodoxy, its star was the most important literary figure in America, capable of finding for his colleagues both lecture invitations and publishing opportunities. Thoreau regularly benefited from these advantages, as well as from a rigorously classical Harvard education. Transcendentalism's house journal, the *Dial,* the new Boston publishing houses, and the emerging Lyceum lecture circuit offered Thoreau and his colleagues new avenues for distribution of their work, and Emerson, combining the roles of critic and artist, was using his famous essays (*Nature,* "The American Scholar," "The Divinity School Address," "Self-Reliance") to proclaim the new critical idea: the emergence of native individualist for whom the natural world would become the means of joy and wisdom.

Given this elaborate support structure, the most well developed of any in the New World, how could Thoreau have failed to achieve something at least approximating Emerson's contemporary success? What went wrong? Why couldn't he reduce the gap and make a living as a writer? The reasons are both subtle and many. For a start, although nominally associated with transcendentalism, Thoreau quickly began to distance himself from that movement's ideas, preferring to experience and describe nature rather than to use it as a symbol of something "higher." His friendship with Emerson cooled, especially after the older man had encouraged Thoreau to undertake the disastrous subvention of the *Week*. The *Dial*'s closure and his own unpopularity as a lecturer shut off commercial avenues, and although Emerson's work seemed to articulate precisely the critical idea that would make sense of Thoreau, even *Walden* breaks up on the high-toned rocks of Emerson's abstractions. In his own journals, Emerson never mentions the book. Although Thoreau seems to have understood the role of publicity—the twenty-six-month stay in the woods was a dramatic way of calling attention to himself—he never managed to articulate a critical idea that would have made his new forms of writing acceptable. What would that idea have been? In the twentieth century, *Walden*'s growing influence often derived from Thoreau's connections to civil rights and environmentalism. In his own century, he was regarded as Emerson's lesser satellite. As a prototype of the avant-garde artist, he stubbornly refused to weave baskets, or write books, that his audience would buy, retreating to the privacy of his two-million-word journal and his solitary walks. He could not close the gap that kept him from earning his living as a writer, but he has become the most important nineteenth-century American writer still read outside the classroom, as Emerson is not. Like Stendhal, he drew a winning lottery ticket.

5.

BOOKS

> There are probably words addressed to our condition exactly,
> which, if we could really hear and understand, would be more
> salutary than the morning or spring to our lives, and possibly put
> a new aspect on the face of things for us. How many a man has
> dated a new era in his life from the reading of a book. (76)

For Thoreau, the book that marked "a new era in his life" was
Emerson's *Nature,* published in the fall of 1836 and checked out of the
Harvard library by Thoreau the following spring. He was ready for
it: having been examined by Emerson on rhetoric in 1835, he had by
1837 won the older man's support for some of Harvard's prize money.
More importantly, Emerson's "manifesto of transcendentalism"
suited Thoreau's interest in reconciling his own avidity for nature
with an emerging intellectual ambition. In *Walden*'s terms, Thoreau
was "a prepared field."

Although he writes dismissively of his own college education,
Walden's enormous number of allusions suggests just how bookish
Thoreau was. In fact, as Richardson details, he read omnivorously,
working fluently in the major European languages, as well as Latin
and Greek. But his choice of reading seems strange, perhaps offering a clue to this mysterious man and his mysterious book. Thoreau,
of course, was steeped in the classics, having a special fondness for
Homer, but as he grew older, his taste became less and less literary:
Goethe and Carlyle, yes, but mostly things like books on Eastern
religions, tracts on Canadian history and Indian life, Cato's treatise

on farming, natural history (especially botany), travel books (a guilty pleasure), William Gilpin on landscape painting, the *Jesuit Relations* (forty-one accounts of the Jesuit missions to Canada's Indians), Darwin. Thoreau showed no interest in fiction: although he knew *Robinson Crusoe*, he apparently never read any of his friend Hawthorne's novels. When we remember that Thoreau was born in 1817, four years after *Pride and Prejudice*, the following list of books he appears never to have looked at seems suggestive:

Austen (b. 1775):	*Pride and Prejudice* (1813)
Stendhal (b. 1783):	*Le rouge et le noir* (1831)
Balzac (b. 1799):	*Le père Goriot* (1834)
Dickens (b. 1812):	*Pickwick Papers* (1837), *A Christmas Carol* (1843), *David Copperfield* (1850)
Melville (b. 1819):	*Moby Dick* (1851)
Flaubert (b. 1821):	*Madame Bovary* (1857)

Thoreau, of course, had no ambitions to write fiction, and the novel itself was still a relatively recent invention. But he also cared little about painting or even contemporary poetry. And in "Higher Laws," declaring "I would fain keep sober always," he associates another art with stimulants (opium, wine, coffee, tea) puritanically dismissed: "Even music may be intoxicating" (147) Hence the question: has any other major literary figure ever cared so little about *art*?

Walden's commentators have often portrayed the opening chapter, "Economy," with its insistence on the *practicality* of Thoreau's experiment, as an alibi mounted in response to the "very particular inquiries . . . made by my townsmen concerning my mode of life" (5). In fact, however, Thoreau was never an aesthete. Adept with tools and machinery (he made the family pencil business highly profitable), equipped with what Emerson called "his skill in woodcraft, and his powerful arithmetic," Thoreau did not need to pose as a practical man. As Emerson acknowledged, "He was very competent to live in any part of the world." In that respect, Thoreau had taken to heart the lessons of transcendentalism, a movement always emphasizing self-culture and political activism more than aesthetics. Having acted out Emerson's ideas at Walden, having helped runaway slaves and defended John Brown, having composed one of the world's most important political documents ("Civil Disobedience"), Thoreau might have expected Emerson's unqualified recognition. He did not get it. Significantly, Emerson's harshest criticisms, appearing in, of all places, his eulogy for Thoreau, attacked his protégé for being impractical:

> Had his genius been only contemplative, he had been fitted to his life, but with his energy and practical ability he seemed born for great enterprise and for command: and I so much regret the loss of his rare powers of action, that I cannot help counting it a fault in him that he had no ambition. Wanting this, instead of engineering for all America, he was the captain of a huckleberry party.

Louisa May Alcott, present at Emerson's address, immediately wrote to a friend that it was "not appropriate to the time or place." But Emerson's picture of Thoreau as a dreamy, unworldly figure established an image still hard to resist.

Although Emerson's *Nature* had provided Thoreau with exactly the kind of experience celebrated by the sentence "How many a man has dated a new era in his life from the reading of a book," his struggle with Emerson resulted in part from an ambition to write that book himself. *Walden* was his response. What might such a book do? Thoreau replies, with apparent modesty, that it can "possibly put a new aspect on the face of things for us." In *Walden*'s terms, doing so would mean seeing "necessity" as choice, "economy" as waste, "idleness" as opportunity, "poverty" as freedom. The same life can become either "desperate" or "blessed."

By choosing the word *aspect,* Thoreau anticipates Wittgenstein's famous discussion of the same problem:

> I contemplate a face, and then suddenly notice its likeness to another. I *see* that it has not changed, and yet I see it differently. I call this experience "noticing an aspect."

Wittgenstein further developed his notion of *aspect* around the gestalt example of the duck-rabbit, a drawing capable of being seen in two different ways. Of a viewer who suddenly recognizes the duck, after having previously only noticed the rabbit, Wittgenstein notes,

"The expression of a change of aspect is the expression of a *new* perception," while the object itself remains *unchanged.*

Thoreau clearly wanted *Walden* to effect such an aspect change in his readers. Everything, he insists, is at stake in our ability to learn that lesson. But who are those readers? On the one hand, *Walden*'s regular use of terms like "one," "man," and "mankind" ("But *men* labor under a mistake. The better part of *man* is soon ploughed into the soil for compost" [7]) make the book's most important points seem universally applicable: "If one advances confidently in the direction of his dreams," the "Conclusion" asserts, "and endeavors to live the life he has imagined, he will meet with a success unexpected in common hours" (217). This apodictic tone, recurring throughout *Walden*, marks not a letter to the elect but a sermon to the masses. Thoreau makes some exceptions, admitting that "I do not speak to those who are well-employed . . . but mainly to the mass of men who are discontented" (14), but since Thoreau regards most men as "discontented," the gesture seems rhetorical.

What, however, could Thoreau do with John Field, the "honest, hardworking, but shiftless" Irishman whom he met near Baker Farm (139)? With his wife and "several children," his "ruin" of a house, and his addiction to the luxuries Thoreau had foresworn ("tea and coffee, and butter and milk, and beef"), John Field proved incapable of seeing life's other aspect, although, as Thoreau recalls, "I purposely talked to him as if he were a philosopher, or desired to be one" (140). "The question now arises," Wittgenstein writes,

could there be human beings lacking in the capacity to see something *as something*—and what would that be like? What sort of consequences would it have?—Would this defect be comparable to colour-blindness or to not having absolute pitch?—We will call it "aspect-blindness."

Walden's final paragraph acknowledges this condition ("I do not say that John or Jonathan will realize all this" [224]), but Thoreau usually insists that, as Wittgenstein writes, "seeing an aspect and imagining are subject to the will." Indeed, Thoreau's persistent emphasis on the role of *choice* in our lives resembles Sartre's existentialism: "I know of no more encouraging fact," Thoreau optimistically proclaims, "than the unquestionable ability of man to elevate his life by a conscious endeavor" (64).

But what to do with the John Fields of this world? If Thoreau intended *Walden*'s lesson to have a practical effect on his readers, but it sometimes fails to, does the fault lie with the reader? With the message itself? Or with the message's expression? "The philosopher," Wittgenstein wrote, "strives to find *the liberating word*, that is the word which finally allows us to grasp what it is that has hitherto, imperceptibly, been a burden upon our consciousness." As stirring as *Walden* is, to the extent that it could not cure John Field's "aspect-blindness," Thoreau did not find the universally "liberating word." And he admits as much in his book's final lines: "The light that puts out our eyes is darkness to us. Only that day dawns to which we are awake" (224). What sort of consequences, Wittgenstein asks, would this blindness have? One of *Walden*'s most famous phrases offers Thoreau's answer: "Lives of quiet desperation" (8).

(with Ryan Hopper and Robert McDonald)

6.

COLORS

"Colours spur us to philosophize," Wittgenstein once observed, but what are to make of Thoreau's prodigality with them? In "The Ponds," he begins a description of Walden by casually remarking that "All our Concord waters have two colors at least, one when viewed at a distance, and another, more proper, close at hand" (121). He doesn't leave the matter there. The ensuing paragraph assembles twenty-nine separate mentions of color to suggest how the neighboring ponds and rivers appear under different conditions and from different perspectives: *blue, dark slate-color, green, as green as grass, the color of the sky, a yellowish tint, light green, uniform dark green, vivid green, verdure, blue mixed with yellow, the color of its iris, a darker blue than the sky itself, a matchless and indescribable blue, more cerulean than the sky itself, original dark green, muddy, vitreous greenish blue, colorless . . . as . . . air, green tint, black or very dark brown, a yellowish tinge, alabaster whiteness.*

In one sense, Thoreau's seems to have anticipated Wittgenstein's point that color words impose *our* sense on the world; they do not simply designate preexisting qualities. Nevertheless, the passage is disconcerting because Thoreau typically offers Walden as the symbol of an ideal permanence, a remainder even of a prelapsarian world:

Perhaps on that spring morning when Adam and Eve were driven out of Eden Walden Pond was already in existence, and even then breaking up in a gentle spring rain accompanied by mist and a southerly wind, and covered with myriads of ducks and geese, which had not heard of the fall. (123)

Recalling childhood visits prompts another celebration of the pond's constancy:

> Of all the characters I have known, perhaps Walden wears best, and best preserves its purity. . . . Though the woodchoppers have laid bare first this shore and then that, and the Irish have built their sties by it, and the railroad has infringed on its border, and the ice-men have skimmed it once, it is itself unchanged, the same water which my youthful eyes fell on; all the change is in me. (132)

But if the pond can assume entirely different colorings, then Thoreau's central image of stability has itself become profoundly *unstable*; and if Walden is unstable, what in Thoreau's book is not? This question gets at one of *Walden*'s central difficulties: the book seems unwilling to settle for either straightforward factual recording or aggressive transcendentalist symbol making. And even when Thoreau does insist on making a natural phenomenon stand for something, he can't decide what that something should be. On the one hand, the pond's flickering, variable coloring is an image of nature in constant flux. On the other, the same pond's resistance to the changes brought by men suggests the truth Thoreau found in Virgil's descriptions of ripening vines and fruit trees: "It was the same world."

Wittgenstein used colors to demonstrate that a word can have meaning even in the absence of a readily available verbal definition. If, for example, someone asks, "What does *red* mean?" we will usually point to a series of red objects, not offer a dictionary's explanation. As Severin Schroeder puts it, "Colour-words . . . are not explained by paraphrase, but by ostension." And so, too, are the things that Thoreau values—the pond, the woods, the seasonal changes, his own exalted moods. Like the color words we know perfectly well how to use, these things resist verbal definition. "This is *red*," we might say, pointing to an apple or a rose or a Vermont barn. "This was my life at Walden Pond, and how I lived there," Thoreau tells us, gesturing toward both the world that he found and the one that he made.

(with Brenda Maxey-Billings)

D

7.

DEATH

Walden lives up almost entirely to the purpose Thoreau announces in the epigraph: "I do not intend to write an ode to dejection." (5) However varied his moods may have been during the book's nine-year gestation, Thoreau produced a consistently optimistic work by sticking to a strict compositional plan: "I put the best face on the matter." As a result, in the midst of so much high spirits, the famous penultimate paragraph of "Where I Lived and What I lived For" seems not only obscure but unexpected:

> If you stand right fronting and face to face to a fact, you will see the sun glimmer on both its surfaces, as if it were a cimiter, and feel its sweet edge dividing you through the heart and marrow, and so you will happily conclude your mortal career. Be it life or death, we crave only reality. If we are really dying, let us hear the rattle in our throats and feel cold in the extremities; if we are alive, let us go about our business. (70)

Thoreau had written like this before. Using the same odd phrase, "to front a fact," he had previously imagined his enterprise as another kind of life-and-death struggle:

> The frontiers are not east or west, north or south, but wherever a man *fronts* a fact, though that fact be his neighbor, there is an unsettled wilderness between him and Canada, between him and the setting sun, or further still, between him and it. Let him build

a log-house with the bark on where he is, *fronting* IT, and wage there an Old French war for seven or seventy years, with Indians and Rangers, or whatever else may come between him and the reality, and save his scalp if he can. (*Week*, 304)

The two passage's similarities, the verbal and thematic repetitions—if these things weren't enough, Geoffrey O'Brien observes that "when Thoreau combines italic and upper-case letters in a single phrase, you know that a critical juncture has been reached." But why would Thoreau include this apocalyptic passage, with its evocation of the death rattle, in *Walden*?

Almost every study of Thoreau treats as decisive his older brother's sudden death from tetanus in January 1842. Indeed, the "private business" (17) Thoreau announces as the purpose of his Walden experiment was initially the completion of *A Week on the Concord and Merrimack Rivers,* intended as a memorial to John, with whom he had taken that canoe trip. John had been only twenty-six when he died, and Thoreau had been so stricken with grief that he had developed psychosomatic lockjaw, complete with all the apparently fatal symptoms. In 1849, Thoreau also watched his thirty-six-year-old sister Helen slowly die from tuberculosis, the family disease that would eventually kill him. These events encouraged a new urgency in Thoreau, imposing an existential imperative to settle once and for all what really mattered to him. Almost seventy years earlier, Samuel Johnson had offered his famous dictum, "When a man knows he is to be hanged in a fortnight, it concentrates his mind wonderfully." Thoreau wasn't going to be hanged, but having seen up close how short a life could be, he went to Walden determined "to live deliberately, to front only the essential facts of life" (that phrase again) and "see if I could not learn what it had to teach, and not, when I came to die, discover that I had not lived" (65).

Thoreau's acquaintance with death almost certainly prompted the intensity of *Walden*'s opening chapters, written as he was finishing the *Week* and thus preoccupied by John's memory. The stirring clarion phrases, designed to wake himself and his neighbors up, issue from the Thoreau who once defined as "good" those "sentences uttered with your back to the wall" (*J*, 12 November 1851):

But men labor under a mistake. . . . [T]hey are employed, as it says in an old book, laying up treasures which moth and rust will corrupt and thieves break through and steal. It is a fool's life, as they will find when they get to the end of it. (7)

What a man thinks of himself, that it is which determines, or rather indicates, his fate. . . . As if you could kill time without injuring eternity. (8)

In the long run men hit only what they aim at. Therefore, though they should fail immediately, they had better aim at something high. (21–22)

The cost of a thing is the amount of what I will call life which is required to be exchanged for it, immediately or in the long run. (24)

The universe constantly and obediently answers to our conceptions; whether we travel fast or slow, the track is laid for us. Let us spend our lives in conceiving then. (69)

This kind of sentence—imposing, insistent, epigrammatic—is what people remember about *Walden*. The predominant tone is *urgency*, as if Thoreau were writing under a sentence of death, with absolutely no time to spare.

But at some point during his experiment, Thoreau seems to have discovered that although an awareness of mortality quickens the appreciation of life ("Death is the mother of beauty," in Wallace Stevens's words), happiness does not depend on living as if you were going to die tomorrow. As this realization sinks in, *Walden*'s pitch becomes less shrill, and its imperative haste gives way to something calmer and more meditative. "When we are unhurried and wise," Thoreau says, announcing this new disposition, "we perceive that only great and worthy things have any permanence and absolute existence." And in case we might suspect a mere falling off of energy, he adds the new lesson: "This is always exhilarating and sublime" (68).

8.

DISTANCE

Despite its reputation as a remote sanctuary, Thoreau's cabin was only a mile and a half from Emerson's door, less than a mile and three quarters from his own family's house, and barely six hundred yards from the Fitchburg railroad's tracks. To what extent does this proximity to the very civilization disowned by *Walden* invalidate the book? If Stanley Cavell is right that Thoreau's "problem is not to learn what to say to his neighbors" but "his right to declare it," is that right undermined by the surprising lack of distance between him and his neighbors?

For some *Walden* readers, captivated by the idea of a heroic retreat from society, the discovery that Thoreau walked into town almost daily, often dined at home, and regularly entertained visitors seems a betrayal. Thoreau, of course, anticipates that response, insisting that the distance that matters is the one separating us from our better selves and that bridging this gulf requires the real heroism. "Is not our own interior white on the chart?" he asks in his "Conclusion," urging his reader to "be a Columbus to whole new continents and worlds within you, opening new channels, not of trade, but of thought" (215). Wittgenstein would propose the same project in the same terms: "If you want to go down deep you do not need to travel far; indeed, you don't have to leave your most immediate and familiar surroundings."

Nevertheless, Thoreau must have remained aware that his physical proximity to Concord might discredit his experiment. Eager to avoid appearing like a boy camping out, he paints a bolder self-portrait:

Where I lived was as far off as many a region viewed nightly by astronomers. We are wont to imagine rare and delectable places in some remote and more celestial corner of the system. . . . I discovered that my house actually had its site in such a withdrawn, but forever new and unprofaned, part of the universe. . . . at an equal remoteness from the life which I had left behind, dwindled and twinkling with as fine a ray to my nearest neighbor, and to be seen only in moonless nights by him. (63)

There is some truth to this picture. In the middle of the nineteenth century, long before the comforting electric glow that now comes from the nearby village, Walden's woods on a moonless night would have seemed impenetrably dark. Returning to his cabin after an evening in town, Thoreau reports having "to feel with my feet the faint track which I had worn," for "it is darker in the woods, even in common nights, than most suppose" (117). In choosing solitude, Thoreau had further made himself exceptional: in 1850, only thirteen of Concord's twenty-three hundred residents were living by themselves, nearly all widows or spinsters, alone out of necessity rather than choice.

And yet the distance problem—or rather the lack of it—remains. It's hard to think of another major American literary work capable of being so easily discredited by information about its author. *Huckleberry Finn* doesn't become a lesser book when we discover that Twain wrote it in Hartford; *The Red Badge of Courage* doesn't collapse because Stephen Crane hadn't experienced combat. Only Hemingway and Frost, who worked so hard to make their books seem extensions of their lives, come anywhere close to being as vulnerable. "Thoreau's work disconcerts most by its lack of clear boundaries," Geoffrey O'Brien argues. "You begin by reading a book and find that you have crossed over into a life." But surely that diagnosis does not apply only to *Walden*: it would describe almost any memoir purporting to be truthful. Thoreau's distance problem, in other words, is a *genre* issue, responsive to an easy remedy: if he had called *Walden* "a novel," no one would care how often he went to town. Simply designating any account as "fictional" erects a protective bulkhead between the work and its author: think how often faked holocaust memoirs get "cured" by being renamed "novels."

But Thoreau wouldn't take the easy way out, and he had his reasons. "I never read a novel," he once declared. "They have so little real life and thought in them." He was willing to hold himself to the standard laid out on *Walden*'s first page: "I, on my side, require of every writer, first or last, a simple and sincere account of his own life, and not merely what he has heard of other men's lives" (5). His book fudges on some things: it tells us that "I wrote the following pages, or rather the bulk of them" at the cabin (he didn't); that his second year in the woods "was similar" to his first (it wasn't, at least not entirely); except in *Walden*'s first sentence, he rarely mentions how much time he spent writing. Yet his book survives, and despite the famous cabin's proximity to Concord, Thoreau's example remains inspiring, forbidding, *remote*.

9.

DRUMMER

Why should we be in such desperate haste to succeed, and in such desperate enterprises? If a man does not keep pace with his companions, perhaps because it is because he hears a different drummer. Let him step to the music which he hears, however measured or far away. (219)

Thoreau has always managed to provoke distinguished writers to criticism. Exasperated by Thoreau's preachy austerity, Hawthorne complained that "one feels ashamed to have any money, or a house to live in, or so much as two coats to wear." A disappointed Emerson characterized the man assumed to be his best friend as difficult to like, reflexively contentious, and without ambition or literary talent. Three years after Thoreau's death, James Russell Lowell emphasized his humorlessness and egoism and proposed that his books should have been shorter: "He registers the state of his personal thermometer thirteen times a day." Henry James found the effect of Thoreau's work diminished by "eccentricity" and observed that "it is only at his best that he is readable." Robert Louis Stevenson called him a "prig" and a "skulker" and objected to his self-indulgent remoteness from even his friends: "A man who must separate himself from his neighbors' habits in order to be happy, is in much the same case with one who requires to take opium for the same purpose."

Doubts about Thoreau usually begin with the attitude expressed by this famous passage, which in its popular variant, now part of the language, celebrates the individual who "marches to the beat of a different drummer." Thoreau's adamantine individualism would make friendship difficult and civilization impossible. Stevenson reprovingly cited Thoreau's reply to a simple invitation—"*Such are my engagements to myself* that I dare not promise"—to suggest how extreme his commitment to himself became. Emerson lamented that "instead of engineering for all America, he was the captain of a huckleberry party." After all, if everyone hears a different drummer, you can't have a parade.

This objection (usually taking the form of a question: "What if *everyone* lived like this?") had been raised in the eighteenth century by Voltaire in his comments on Pascal's *Pensées*. When unattributed, many of Pascal's remarks can often seem like a *Walden* passage you must somehow have missed: "All of man's unhappiness comes from the fact that he is unable to sit quietly by himself in a room." Voltaire, however, would have none of it: "What would a man be," he asks, "who should remain in a state of inactivity, and be supposed to contemplate himself? I affirm such a person would not only be an idiot, a useless member of society, but I will also as boldly affirm, that no such man can ever exist." Voltaire confronted Pascal's celebration of the mystical with an insistence on practicality. Individual genius, he argued, could not be allowed to override social custom; action is more valuable than contemplation. Against Pascal's Thoreauvian insistence on the present, Voltaire asserted a reality test: "Were mankind so unhappy as to employ their minds only on the time present, no person would sow, build, plant, or make the least provision." Voltaire's rejection of Pascal encourages the recognition that Thoreau's "Economy" poses "the paradox of thrift": although individual frugality is admirable, when everyone stops spending, the economy goes into free fall.

Thoreau, of course, sat on both sides of the Pascal-Voltaire debate: he was at once the most spiritually alert and the most practically adept man in Concord. That combination accounts for his inconsistencies. Before *Walden*, for example, he had already used the image of a distant drummer to celebrate not a belligerent individualism but a genial community. In the *Week*, as he and his brother lay falling asleep beside the Merrimack, they heard "far in the night" the sounds of an inexperienced drummer practicing a county muster. And Thoreau seemed willing to fall in: "We could have assured him that his beat would be answered, and the forces be mustered. Fear not, thou drummer of the night, we too will be there" (*Week*, 173). This last sentence, of course, is typical Thoreauvian hyperbole, occasioned less by conviction than rhetoric. "Thoreau was an exaggerative and a parabolical writer," Stevenson observed, and he could use the sound of a different drummer to make two very different points. He didn't join up in the *Week*, and *Walden* makes clear that he never had any intentions of doing so.

For all of Thoreau's austere, and sometimes strident, individuality, he is recognizable as a *type*, one described by Nietzsche in a passage that exactly accords with the descriptions of Thoreau that have come down to us, both his own and those of the people who knew him:

> Free-spirited people, living for knowledge alone, will soon find that they have achieved their external goal in life, their ultimate position vis à vis society and the state, and gladly be satisfied, for example, with a minor position or a fortune that just meets their needs; for they will set themselves up to live in such a way that a great change in economic conditions, even a revolution in political structures, will not overturn their life with it. They expend as little energy as possible on all these things, so that they can plunge with all their assembled energy, as if taking a deep breath, into the element of knowledge. They can then hope to dive deep, and also get a look at the bottom. . . .
>
> He, too, knows the week-days of bondage, dependence, and service. But from time to time he must get a Sunday of freedom, or else he will not endure life.
>
> It is probable that even his love of men will be cautious and somewhat short-winded.

"What if everyone lived like that?" Nietzsche called that prospect "the greatest danger," and he also used a musical metaphor to make the point. Because "man's greatest labor so far has been to reach agreement about very many things," the eruption of radical individualism, with its attendant "arbitrariness in feeling, seeing, and hearing," threatens everything:

> What is needed is *virtuous stupidity*, stolid metronomes for the slow spirit, to make sure that the faithful of the great shared faith

stay together and continue their dance. It is a first-rate need that commands and demands this. *We others are the exception and the danger*—and we need eternally to be defended.—Well, there actually are things to be said in favor of the exception, *provided that it never wants to become the rule.*

"I would not have any one adopt *my* mode of living on any account," Thoreau advises, anticipating Nietzsche's warning. But he immediately resumes his typical stance, which would make society impossible: "I would have each one be very careful to find out and pursue *his own* way, and not his father's or his mother's or his neighbor's instead" (52). Without a metronome, each of us would need his own drum.

E

10

EXPERIMENT

Here is life, an experiment to a great extent untried by me. (9)

But to make haste to my own experiment. (31)

The present was my next experiment of this kind, which I purpose to describe more at length; for convenience, putting the experience of two years into one. (60)

We are the subjects of an experiment which is not a little interesting to me. (94)

Thoreau's preferred term for his twenty-six months at the pond is *experiment*, a word that appears throughout *Walden*. How would *Walden*'s meaning change if he had described his activities differently?

   1. *Adventure* is a word Thoreau does, in fact, use early in "Economy," insisting that with basic needs satisfied, a man should "adventure on life" (14). Thoreau may have sensed, however, that to the extent that the word evokes *Robinson Crusoe* and boys' books, it would trivialize his own story. And there was another problem. Since his first audience of Concord neighbors knew that, in words cited by William E. Cain, "Thoreau 'really lived at home, where he went every day', while he 'bivoucked' at his cabin," they might have laughed at any attempt to describe his puzzling activities with so heroic a word as *adventure*.

2. *Experience* is a word Thoreau often uses , as in this passage from "Economy":

I learned from my two years' experience that it would cost incredibly little trouble to obtain one's necessary food, even in this latitude. (45)

Experience is a mild word compared to *experiment,* but one that the French-speaking Thoreau would have recognized as having both meanings in that language (*expérience*).

3. *Trip* would suggest a travel book, a genre loved by Thoreau, and its connotation, a voyage of (self-)discovery, is often exploited by *Walden*. But having taken up residence only a little over a mile from his family home, Thoreau had not really gone on a trip.

4. *Stay* is a neutral word, implying a more passive twenty-six months than Thoreau wished to convey.

5. *Sojourn,* a word, meaning "a temporary stay" but also implying a kind of willed exile, seems perfect, but Thoreau uses it in *Walden*'s first paragraph to describe what he actually regards as provisional, his renewed residence in *civilization*. Thoreau, as Paul Johnson puts it, "exiled himself back into society."

6. *Residence,* a word evoking permanence and civilization, would undercut Thoreau's desire to portray his enterprise as an exploration.

Experiment, of course, with its scientific connotation, makes Thoreau's stay in the woods seem less eccentric and capricious than rigorous and methodical. Although Thoreau inherited romanticism's devotion to a spiritualized "Nature," his interest in science was genuine. Wordsworth had characterized scientific reasoning as "that false secondary power/By which we multiply distinctions" (*The Prelude* 2.216–17), but *Walden* represents an attempt to overcome the split between science and poetry, reason and intuition, practicality and imagination. The word *experiment* does a lot of work for Thoreau, endowing his project with the kind of hard-earned credibility he often found lacking in Emerson.

A scientific experiment begins with a hypothesis designed to address a problem. By going to Walden, Thoreau hoped to solve several specific problems of his own, beginning with a vocational crisis. He had proved unsuited to teaching, and the poetry and essays he had begun writing would have become profitable only if they had enabled the kind of Lyceum lecturing from which Emerson earned so much of his income. Thoreau, however, was never Emerson's peer as a lecturer, and thus, he seemed stuck with odd jobs and the family's pencil business, which he ran successfully without enjoying it. In fact, Thoreau chafed at almost any kind of regular work except writing. "I love a broad margin to my life," Thoreau announces, describing a summer morning when "I sat in my sunny doorway from sunrise till noon, rapt in a revery," precisely the kind of experience he valued but one which, he conceded, "was sheer idleness to my fellow-townsmen" (79). Even intellectual work like lecturing seemed a distraction: "The lecturer gets fifty dollars a night," he wrote to Harrison Blake, "but what becomes of his winter? . . . I should like not to exchange *any* of my life for money."

Thoreau's third letter to Blake had already set the problem: "How shall we earn our bread is a grave question. . . . It is the most important and practical question which is put to man." In one sense, like many people, Thoreau simply wanted a way of supporting himself that would not take up too much of his time. But his own vocational anxiety also reflected Emerson's portrayal of this moment as decisive. "All Emerson's young men had trouble in choosing careers," Sherman Paul observes. "The point at which a society bears down on an individual is in the choice of vocation: here is the battlefield of values and the gamble for rewards." Paul attributes Thoreau's "lifelong postponing of a recognized vocation" as a means of dodging society's "pressures." Emerson had posed the vocational problem existentially. In "Literary Ethics," an 1838 address to Dartmouth College seniors, he urged that "the hour of that choice is the crisis of your history, and see that you hold yourselves fast by the intellect." Thoreau absorbed both of those lessons.

The Walden experiment proposed to solve a two-part problem: how to make a living, and how to make a life. Thoreau begins with his famous hypothesis: if he could reduce his needs ("Simplify, simplify" [65]), he could spend less time working and more time living. His retreat to the woods became the method for distinguishing between the essential and the frivolous:

It would be some advantage to live a primitive and frontier life, though in the midst of an outward civilization, if only to learn what are the gross necessaries of life. (11)

Following Thomas Carlyle advice to "reduce the denominator"—that is, minimize the needs that consume our income—Thoreau planted beans, wore old clothes, built his own cabin, and practiced a life of such austerity that "I found, that by working about six weeks in a year, I could meet all the expenses of living" (50). He proposes this lesson as generally applicable: "It is not necessary that a man should earn his living by the sweat of his brow, unless he sweats easier than I do" (52). And he reports his experiment's results:

I learned this, at least, by my experiment; that if one advances confidently in the direction of his dreams, and endeavors to live the life which he has imagined, he will meet with success unexpected in common hours. (217)

Walden also represents the outcome of another kind of experiment, one having to do with the activity that occupied Thoreau more than other during his stay at the pond—writing. Here the problem concerned the ideal mode for Thoreau's talents and ambition. He was neither a novelist nor a playwright nor a successful poet. He was not a conventional sermonizer or nature writer. What form could he devise, and what experiment did he undertake? Citing Claude Bernard's notion that "to experiment is to do violence to the object," Daniel S. Milo has suggested that all such experimenting involves at least one of the following procedures: "*adding* to X an element Y which is foreign to it; *removing* from X an element X1 that usually helps constitute it; and *changing the scale:* to observe and analyze X on a scale against which it isn't usually measured." *Walden* enacts such a provoked experiment by "doing violence" to traditional genres.

From the adventure-travel-discovery genre, *Walden* removes the crucial item of *distance*—the pond was too close to Concord for this kind of book. Thoreau also omits any real sense of *danger,* at least of the external sort. Thus, from this perspective, *Walden* is a failed adventure-travel-discovery story. Thoreau, however, has an answer. The real journey, the real frontier is internal: since "our own interior

[is] white on the chart," the demand is for a different kind of under-taking. "Be a Columbus to whole new continents and worlds within you, opening new channels, not of trade, but of thought" (215). And this voyage, Thoreau insists, requires real bravery: "Explore thy-self. Herein are demanded the eye and the nerve. Only the defeated and the deserters go to the wars, cowards that run away and enlist" (216). Thoreau, in other words, also *adds* something to the genre, the notion of the spiritual quest, which adventure stories rarely include. The goal becomes not to discover some physical place like California or Peru but to lose ourselves (117) in order to awake to the wonders around us. Thus, when he writes that "these experiences were very memorable and valuable to me" (120), it's not because they led him to gold or a new continent but because they enabled him to see that "heaven is under our feet as well as over our heads" (190). Evok-ing Charles Dana's *Two Years before the Mast*, precisely the kind of travel-adventure book *Walden* is not, Thoreau shows how he can use that genre's vocabulary for other purposes:

I did not wish to take a cabin passage, but to go before the mast and on the deck of the world, for there I could best see the moonlight amid the mountains. I do not wish to go below now. (217)

As Stephen Fender has pointed out, *Walden* also has elements in com-mon with another genre, self-help books on progressive farming, home economics, and continuing education. But Thoreau *removes* from this genre its practicality. His own accounts are hopeless: to build his cabin, he overpays for the other cottage's boards, and he never acknowledges the land's value or its taxes or his own labor. His famous beans were, in fact, an undesirable crop; he planted the seed too late and set them too far apart in unfertilized soil. Even more importantly, Thoreau undermines the basic principle of self-help literature, that discipline and work provide the keys to success. "We are made to exaggerate the importance of what work we do" (11), he insists, introducing a book where salvation often seems to depend on a kind of alert loafing, as is suggested in a fuller version of the passage cited before:

There were times when I could not afford to sacrifice the bloom of the present moment to any work, whether of the head or hands. I love a broad margin to my life. Sometimes, in a summer morning, having taken my accustomed bath, I sat in my sunny doorway from sunrise till noon, rapt in a revery, amidst the pines and sumachs, in undisturbed solitude and stillness. . . . I grew in these seasons like corn in the night, and they were far better than any work of the hands would have been. (79)

In moments like this one, *Walden* seems to anticipate André Breton's conclusion in *Nadja:* "The event from which each of us is entitled to expect the revelation of his own life's meaning . . . *is not earned by work.*"

Furthermore, as a self-help book, *Walden's* scale is off. The mock-scrupulous calculation of expenses to the quarter of a penny, the meticulous dating of the pond's freezing and melting, the exact registering of seasonal changes—these signals confirm Geoffrey O'Brien's observation that Thoreau's "genius lies in getting stuck on the simplest point, poking at one query until it gives birth to a thousand others." Like someone who repeats a familiar word over and over until it becomes strange, Thoreau keeps looking at himself and the woods and the way we live until a new kind of question presents itself: "Why do precisely these objects which we behold make a world?" (153). Thoreau's answer lies in what he *adds* to the self-help genre—not the usual secrets for getting rich, planting corn, or building a house but something else. If you follow *Walden's* instructions, Thoreau advises, you will see that "God himself culminates in the present moment" (69), even if that moment is in "this restless, nervous, bustling, trivial Nineteenth Century" (221). If we believe him, *Walden* is not only an experiment but a proof.

(with Paul Johnson, Alison Meyer, and Michael Pitt)

11.

FASHION

"Economy"'s review of life's necessities—food, clothing, shelter—quickly becomes Thoreau's occasion for dismissing fashion: "As for Clothing . . . , we are led oftener by the love of novelty, and a regard for the opinions of men, in procuring it, than by a true utility" (18). Although this proto-Marxist critique of exchange-value initially appears as simply part of Thoreau's recipe for improving our condition by reducing our needs, his later declaration that "our whole life is startlingly moral" (148) confirms *Walden*'s insistence on erasing the practical/moral distinction so eagerly maintained by Concord's Sunday churchgoing businessmen. Hence the constant slippage between economic and spiritual terms, whose overlap appears in one of Thoreau's favorite words: *value.* Hence, too, the immediate mobilization of fashion's ethical dimension: "I am sure that there is greater anxiety, commonly, to have fashionable, or at least clean and unpatched clothes, than to have a sound conscience" (18).

Walden argues that the enormous effort involved in being fashionable wastes *time,* always for Thoreau our most valuable possession. Having determined that "the cost of a thing is the amount of what I will call life which is required to be exchanged for it, immediately or in the long run" (24), he concludes that "the only cure" for discontent and desperation" lies with "a rigid economy, a stern and more than Spartan simplicity of life and elevation of purpose" (66). This "rigid economy" would discourage architecture, a field that arose out of an unnecessary division of labor, turning house building into a specialized profession and encouraging the ascendancy of useless decoration. "A great proportion of architectural ornaments are literally hollow," Thoreau observes, "and a September gale would strip them off, like borrowed plumes, without injury to the substantials. They can do without *architecture* who have no olives nor wines in the cellar" (36). Again, the characteristic slide between two registers, the practical and the moral: "Before we can adorn our houses with beautiful objects the walls must be stripped, and our lives must be stripped (29).

Thoreau does not exempt literature from this critique:

> What if an equal ado were made about the ornaments of style in literature, and the architects of our bibles spent as much time about their cornices as the architects of our churches do? So are made the *belles-lettres* and the *beaux-arts* and their professors. (36)

If this remark represents Thoreau's casual, perverse philistinism, it also betrays a blindness about his own project. For *Walden*, of course, everywhere depends on precisely the kind of belle-lettristic ornament that it denounces. With its puns, metaphors, similes, allusions, invented etymologies, adjectival richness, and epigrammatic flourish, *Walden*'s prose is hardly "stripped." (It would take Hemingway to accomplish that feat.) The famous directive to "Simplify, simplify," for example, is followed almost immediately by a sentence of eighty-five words (65–66)! What, in any case, would a purely "functional" *Walden* look like? An instruction manual? Although Thoreau's book has something in common with that genre, the differences make *Walden* literature.

Nevertheless, Thoreau's attack on fashion cannot be easily dismissed. In fact, even in its details, it anticipates Adolf Loos's famous 1908 essay, "Ornament and Crime," the manifesto that would inspire the Bauhaus and architectural modernism. Like Thoreau, Loos would see that the "capital outlay" required by fashion left its devotés poorer than those who managed to ignore it. Loos would also argue that fashion's burdens fell disproportionately on women, who became not only its objects but also its laborers, paid "criminally low wages." *Walden* had made the same point, noting that "clothes introduced sewing, a kind of work which you may call endless; a woman's dress, at least, is never done" (19). "*The evolution of culture is synonymous with the removal of ornament from utilitarian objects,"* Loos would declare. Ornament is "a waste of human labor, money, and material"; it is a vestige of a primitive eroticism that we have outgrown or, rather, that we *must* outgrow. For like Thoreau, Loos is less cultural critic than moralist. "Freedom from ornament," he would conclude, "is a sign of spiritual strength."

In associating ornament with the primitive (the "Papuan," who eats his enemies and "tattoos his skin, his boat, his paddles, in short everything he can lay his hands on"), Loos would repeat the terms of Thoreau's denunciation of fashion, defined in *Walden* as "the childish and savage taste of men and women for new patterns" (21). In fact, Loos was appropriating the genealogy of Auguste Comte's positivism, the nineteenth century's most influential philosophy. Comte had proposed that all civilizations evolve from infantile "theological" and adolescent "metaphysical" stages to the final maturity of "positivism." If the theologian attributes a burning bush to God's presence, and the metaphysician uses unexamined abstractions like "phlogisten," a positivist looks for a match. Even in Thoreau's lifetime, this scheme, where later is better, had begun to serve as European imperialism's principal ethical justification: "mature" civilizations were simply making infantile ones "grow up."

Thoreau's disdain for fashion would reemerge in Wittgenstein, who similarly restricted himself to a basic diet, plain clothes, and undecorated furniture and who designed a house in Vienna for his sister that remains a monument to the severest architectural austerity. More important, the repudiation of ornament would emerge as a philosophical theme, with Wittgenstein's *Tractatus* dismissing nonsensical metaphysical speculation in favor of a mathematically functional logic. "The world is everything that is the case," that book begins, as if to answer Thoreau's enchanted question, "Why do precisely these objects which we behold make a world?" (153).

To what extent does Thoreau's attack on fashion symptomize an increasing discomfort with transcendentalism? An 1856 letter to B. B. Wiley sounds the explicit notes of positivism: "I do not now remember anything which Confucius has said directly regarding man's 'origin, purpose, and destiny,'" he writes dismissively. "He was more practical than that." Published two years earlier, *Walden* is a halfway house, located between Emerson's high-toned abstractions and the

Journal's eventual near-total commitment to factual annotation. In the *Week*, Thoreau had reached a similar compromise, writing that "there are various tough problems yet to solve, and we must shift to live, betwixt spirit and matter, such a human life as we can" (73–74). But as he withdrew into the woods, and as *Walden's* interior chapters increasingly replaced moralizing with description, eliminating narration almost completely, Thoreau must have known he was writing a deliberately *unfashionable* book, even if he could not have foreseen that it would require over half a century to find its audience.

(with Lauren Lester and Carly Roach)

12.

FLUTE

In warm evenings I frequently sat in the boat playing the flute. (120)

And now to-night my flute has waked the echoes over that very water. (107)

Although Thoreau's intermittent moralizing could make him denounce music as "intoxicating," grouping it with wine, liquor, coffee, and tea ("Ah, how low I feel when I am tempted by them! [147]), he, like his father and brother, played the flute, and he took his instrument with him to Walden. We even know his favorite song: "Tom Bowling," written by Englishman Charles Dibdin (1745–1814), who seems to have specialized in ersatz folk ballads about sailors. Catherine Moseley describes Thoreau's musical taste as "mainstream bourgeois"; he had little interest in what we now call "classical music" but instead preferred "extremely elaborate and sentimental" songs that were excessive and "florid." The same Thoreau who sternly advised "read the best books first, or you may not have the chance to read them at all" (*Week*, 98) enjoyed tunes like "Pilgrim Fathers" and "Evening Bells." In particular, as Moseley points out, "Tom Bowling" "does not seem the likely favorite of one whose cry was 'Simplicity, simplicity, simplicity.'" Susan Sontag once observed that we should not expect anyone to have "good taste" in more than one area. Wittgenstein, for example, who insisted to Bertrand Russell "that nothing is tolerable except producing great works or enjoying those of others," liked Carmen Miranda movies. Nevertheless, because we have grown used to regarding musical preferences as a clue to personality, the knowledge of what Thoreau must have been playing while idling in his boat on the glassy surface of the pond on long summer evenings seems to open a previously undiscovered door.

Thoreau was never indifferent to what he heard, and he was eager to provide *Walden* with a soundtrack. After the book's introductory chapters ("Economy," "Where I Lived and What I Lived For," "Reading"), the first to detail his everyday life in the woods is "Sounds." First-time *Walden* readers are often surprised by how much space that chapter devotes not to natural phenomena but to the rattle and scream of the Fitchburg train that roared past his cabin several times a day. Nevertheless, Thoreau also records the noises made by pigeons, fish hawks, reed birds, a carriage and team, town bells, cows, minstrels, whippoorwills, screech and hooting owls, a wagon crossing a bridge, dogs, bullfrogs, squirrels, blue jays, a hare or woodchuck, geese, loons, and foxes. He does not mention his own flute-playing until later.

Thoreau begins "Sounds" by comparing "written languages" to "the language which all things and events speak without metaphor" (78). Sound, in fact, may communicate more directly than any other medium. Citing filmmaker Robert Bresson, Noël Burch has pointed out that "sound, because of its greater realism, is infinitely more evocative than an image, which is essentially only a stylization of visual reality." Evidence confirms Bresson's insight: a January 1945 live recording of Furtwängler conducting Brahms's Symphony no. 1 in Berlin, with audible coughs from the audience, provides a more urgent sense of being in that concert hall in that ruined city than do films of the same event. More than the music, it's the coughing and shuffling that produce this effect. As Gilberto Perez notes, "The visual scene, however vividly presented, will always tolerate the pastness of a narration; but the moment a character speaks [or a spectator coughs], the action comes to life before us." Thus, if by some miracle, we had a recording of Thoreau playing his flute in the woods, it might bring us closer to his experience than all of "Sounds." The sound would "speak without metaphor."

(with Brenda Maxey-Billings)

13.

FULL OF HOPE

In "Spring," *Walden's* penultimate chapter, Thoreau describes his sudden awareness that winter was finally over:

> The change from storm and winter to serene and mild weather, from dark and sluggish hours to bright and elastic ones, is a memorable crisis which all things proclaim. It is seemingly instantaneous at last. Suddenly an influx of light filled my house, though the evening was at hand, and the clouds of winter still overhung it, and the eaves were dripping with sleety rain. I looked out the window, and lo! where yesterday was cold gray ice there lay the transparent pond already calm and full of hope as on a summer evening. (209)

We can imagine this moment as a film scene, with Thoreau at his window and a point-of-view shot revealing what he sees. The *Walden* passage provides the visual details: the abrupt "influx of light," the overhanging clouds and still-dripping eaves, the pond liberated from its ice. But how does a writer *show* us that something is "full of hope"?

In his essay "What Novels Can Do That Films Can't (and Vice Versa)," Seymour Chatman describes the cinema as denotatively rich and connotatively poor. The camera easily presents what appears before it but struggles to assert its significance. Thus, it can show a thirty-five-year-old woman, but without further (usually verbal) cues, it cannot guarantee that a viewer will immediately grasp her age. (She might, after all, look much older or much younger.) The camera can render "an influx of light," and clouds, and eaves dripping with sleet, but it cannot show "full of hope." A writer, on the other hand, as Robbe-Grillet demonstrated, may expend pages detailing something that a movie could show in single shot. But the writer can also simply assert that "a thirty-five-year-old woman walked into the room," or that a pond looked "full of hope."

Thoreau wanted to be both a presentational and an assertive writer: he insisted on meticulously recording the facts he experienced, but he also needed the reader to know what they meant. In effect, this double ambition makes *Walden* a hybrid book, partly cinematic, partly literary, and its difficulties arise when readers find themselves caught between modes. To approach "Economy," for example, expecting a narrative of Thoreau's first days at the pond will lead to immediate disappointment: it's all assertion and argument. But adapting to that approach leaves the same reader unprepared for the inner chapters' immersion in description that often abandons explicit designations of significance.

Robert Richardson notes that Thoreau's "early efforts at scenic descriptions . . . are remarkably inept. Abstract and wordy, they are loaded with scene-killing comparisons that cannot be visualized." By 1851, Thoreau was reminding himself of the need for "sentences which suggest far more than they say, which have an atmosphere about them" (*J*, 22 August 1851). In effect, he was looking for T. S. Eliot's "objective correlative," a concrete detail capable of producing in a reader the sensations he had experienced in that New England twilight, or, in Eliot's words, "the verbal equivalent for states of mind and feeling." In many ways, he had found it a few pages earlier in a passage about an old hunter at an ice-covered Fair-Haven Pond:

> After he had lain still there about an hour he heard a low and
> seemingly very distant sound, but singularly grand and impressive,
> unlike anything he had ever heard, gradually swelling and increas-
> ing as if it would have a universal and memorable ending, a sullen
> rush and roar, which seemed to him all at once like the sound of
> a vast body of fowl coming in to settle there, and, seizing his gun,
> he started up in haste and excited; but he found, to his surprise,
> that the whole body of the ice had started while he lay there, and

drifted in to the shore, and the sound he had heard was made by its edge grating on the shore,—at first gently nibbled and crumbled off, but at length heaving up and scattering its wrecks along the island to a considerable height before it came to a stand still. (204)

Thoreau is describing a simple phenomenon, the melting ice that signals the arrival of spring. Unlike the "full of hope" passage that follows five pages later, this description comes equipped with no assertions of meaning. Thoreau's dramatic rendering, however, suggests an awakening: after lying dormant beneath the snow and ice, Nature is emerging from its hibernation. As Thoreau grew older, the long New England winters made him increasingly lethargic and melancholy. Like Nature's, his own renewal depended on the spring. With his career having come to an impasse and his friendship with Emerson cooling, Thoreau at twenty-eight must have felt himself frozen as he began his Walden experiment. But if *Walden*'s "Conclusion" represents the thunderous noise of Thoreau's own ice breaking up, it had been melting for some time. Thus, his description of the hunter's ice amounts to a description of himself and the way his moods synchronized with the seasons. His rendering of its sudden melting becomes the premise for the assertion that the pond is "full of hope." Because we've read about another lake shrugging off its ice, we can now "see" what "full of hope" looks like.

(with Craig Cieslikowski and Robert McDonald)

G

14

GENIUS

Although Emerson famously said of Thoreau that "his biography is in his verses," he described those verses as "rude and defective," concluding that Thoreau's "genius was better than his talent." Without citing Emerson as the source of this famous judgment, Henry James extended its application to Thoreau's prose, declaring in 1879 that "whatever question there may be of his talent, there can be none, I think of his genius. . . . He was imperfect, unfinished, inartistic . . . ; it is only at his best that he is readable." Why did Emerson and James arrive at this opinion? What aspects of Thoreau's writing prompted it?

While any list of writers with more talent than genius will always be a long one, the reverse is not the case. What American writers have had more genius than talent? Whitman? Gertrude Stein? Hart Crane? Thomas Wolfe? Has this imbalance occurred more frequently in America? And is it more common with writers, as opposed to other kinds of artists? We can start to answer these questions by noting that an artist needs to be lucky enough to have a genre available to him that suits his genius. Imagine if Larry Hart had come along *before* the flowering of the Broadway musical: he would have become, at best, simply a talented light-verse writer, a reduced version of his own ancestor, Heinrich Heine. Had Elvis Presley arrived before rock and roll, he might have developed into a minor version of his idol, Dean Martin, himself a lesser Sinatra. Elvis, of course, helped to invent the genre his genius required, and his ability to do so suggests a way to think about Thoreau and *Walden*.

Less lucky than Hart and Presley, Thoreau had no talent for poetry or fiction, the available genres, and thus, he routinely struggled to find a mode suitable to his genius, "a very crooked one," he admits (41). He occasionally acknowledged the problem: "We sometimes experience a mere fullness of life, which does not find any channels to flow into," he wrote in his journal. "I feel myself uncommonly prepared for *some* literary work, but I can select no work" (*J*, 7 September 1851). One response to this impasse was a stubborn assertion of independence that anticipates Emerson's criticism: "It is a waste of time for the writer to use his talents merely," Thoreau declared. "Be faithful to your genius. Write in the strain that interests you most. Consult not popular taste" (*J*, 20 December 1851). Thoreau also developed a working method: the "inspirations" entered so freely in his journal were "winnowed into Lectures, and again, in due time, from lectures into essays." The lectures, in turn, became books, but Thoreau himself recognized the problem:

> And at last they stand, like the cubes of Pythagoras, firmly on either basis; like statues on their pedestals, but the statues rarely take hold of hands. There is only such connection and series as is attainable in the galleries. And this affects their immediate practical and popular influence. (*J*, summer 1845)

In his perceptive essay on Thoreau, Robert Louis Stevenson proposed that "the true business of literature is with narrative": "Dry precept and disembodied disquisition, as they can only be read with an effort of abstraction," will never have the effect of a simple anecdote. Because "Thoreau could not clothe his opinions in the garment of art, for that was not his talent," Stevenson diagnosed—because, in other words, he couldn't invent a story—"he sought to gain the same elbow-room for himself, and to afford a similar relief to his readers, by mingling his thoughts with a record of experience." Thus, trying to make his statues hold hands, Thoreau forced the record of his excursions, thoughts, and inspirations into clunky receptacles. The *Week* compresses a two-week trip into one, devoting a chapter to each of the seven days. But the book, as critics have always noted, is really a hodge-podge of journal entries, poems, previously published essays, literary criticism, and nature description. It's a cut-

and-paste collage anticipating both filmmaking and the word processor. As Samuel Johnson said of *Paradise Lost,* "None ever wished it longer." *Walden* subjects its raw material to another procrustean bed, reducing Thoreau's twenty-six-month stay in the woods to a single year and roughly following the seasons. *Walden* also borrows so extensively from Thoreau's poems and journals that relatively few pages from the period between July 1845 and September 1847 remain intact.

In neither case did Thoreau find a readily accessible form matched to his genius. With Walden, however, he accomplished something an existing genre might not have allowed. Thoreau went to the woods to solve at least two problems, one a matter of vocation, the other of writing. His solutions were identical: just as he invented his own profession, he also created his own hybrid form. Walden is the sui generis instance of it.

(with Brenda Maxey-Billings)

15.

GOOD AND EVIL

Here are two passages, one from Thoreau and one from Nietzsche:

The greater part of what my neighbors call good I believe in my soul to be bad, and if I repent of any thing, it is very likely to be my good behavior. (10)

What preserves the species.—The strongest and most evil spirits have so far done the most to advance humanity: again and again they relumed the passions that were going to sleep—all ordered society puts the passions to sleep—and they reawakened again and again the sense of comparison, of contradiction, of the pleasure of what is new, daring, untried; they compelled men to pit opinion against opinion, model against model. Usually by force of arms, by toppling boundary markers, by violating pieties. . . . In every teacher and preacher of what is *new* we encounter the same "wickedness." . . . What is new, however, is always *evil,* being that which wants to conquer and overthrow the old boundary markers and the old pieties; and only what is old is good.

If Thoreau is, in many ways, as radical a thinker as Nietzsche, why do we need comparisons of this sort to remind us? How can we account for the different effect produced by their writings? Nietzsche's notoriety derives largely from his rhetorical choices: hyperbole, ellipsis, metaphor, paradox, compression. Language is "a lie," "What is new . . . is always *evil,*" the Greeks "were superficial—*out of profundity,*" knowledge is "useful error," "God is dead." Thoreau, on the other hand, labored for seven years to construct from journal fragments something at least resembling a coherent argument. In making this compromise, he recognized the dilution of the inspirational rush and the power of facts not yet smothered by moralizing: "Obey the spur of the moment," he wrote to himself (J, 26 January 1852). "Mere facts and names and dates communicate more than we suspect. . . . Is the scholastic air any advantage?" (J, 27 January 1852).

Well, yes, it is. It enabled Thoreau to find a publisher in 1854 New England, while thirty years later, Nietzsche would have trouble doing so in Germany. In private, Thoreau could write as provocatively as Nietzsche: "Do not be too moral," he advised Harrison Blake. "You may cheat yourself out of much life so. Aim above morality." In *Walden*, however, he softens that tone by filling in the argument's steps: "Persevere, even if the world call it doing evil, as it most likely they will" (53). Nietzsche would simply have written, "Persevere in doing evil." The difference is important.

(with Adam Nikolaidis)

16.

HIGHER LAWS

"Higher Laws," a late addition to *Walden,* often presents Thoreau in his least modern, least sympathetic light. After the famous opening confession of his desire "to seize and devour [a woodchuck] raw," accompanied by the appropriate lesson ("I love the wild not less than the good") (145), Thoreau quickly embarks on a series of repudiations: hunting, fishing, animal food ("there is something essentially unclean about this diet and all flesh" [146]), wine, coffee, tea ("Ah, how low I fall when I am tempted by them!"), and even music, which "may be intoxicating" (147). He is only warming up for the big topic. Here is Thoreau singing the virtues of chastity and sounding like *Dr. Strangelove*'s General Ripper, with his talk of "precious bodily fluids":

> We are conscious of an animal in us, which awakens in proportion as our higher nature slumbers. It is reptile and sensual, and perhaps cannot be wholly expelled; like the worms which, even in life and health, occupy our bodies. . . . The generative energy, which when we are loose, dissipates and makes us unclean, when we are continent invigorates and inspires us. Chastity is the flowering of man. (149)

This passage makes it hard to remember that while at Walden, Thoreau was writing *A Week on the Concord and Merrimack Rivers,* with its call for "a purely *sensuous* life" (382), and that as early as 1848, he was advising Harrison Blake, "Do not be too moral. You may cheat yourself out of much life so." With "Higher Laws," however, the *Walden* instruction manual takes a decidedly puritanical turn, and reconciling it with the Thoreau who insists that "we need the tonic of wildness" is probably impossible. Almost certainly, Thoreau's failure to consummate any relationship predisposed him to sexual anxiety, which required resolution in his writing.

Thoreau liked to think of himself as a renegade, escaping the reaches of society. "There is a prairie beyond your laws," he wrote in his journal, during one of *Walden*'s last revisions. "Nature is a prairie for outlaws. There are two worlds, the post-office and nature. I know them both. I continually forget mankind and their institutions, as I do a bank" (*J*, 3 January 1853). Twelve days later, he went further, describing what he expected Nature to provide: "True words . . . , transport, rapture, ravishment, ecstasy. These are the words I want" (*J*, 15 January 1853). Even this entry shouldn't surprise us: the mystical tradition, after all, has regularly deployed sexual terms to approximate its desired state. "Higher Laws" is no exception: "Man flows at once to God when the channel of purity is open" (149).

For Thoreau, "purity" amounts to a state of grace. Whether that state can be *deliberately* achieved is *Walden*'s great question. To a large extent, the *Journal*'s meticulous descriptions amount to a meditative practice designed to enable it. In *Walden*, Thoreau typically keeps the channel of purity open by means other than renunciation. In those places, he seems most himself: delighting "in the intervals of a gentle rain storm in August" (62), taking morning baths in the pond (63), sitting "in my sunny doorway from sunrise till noon" (79), listening to the church bells' echo (87), getting lost in the woods (117), fishing at night (121), standing in a rainbow's arch (138), hearing the boom of the ice's breaking up (202)—"These experiences," he concludes, "were very memorable and valuable to me" (120). For Thoreau, "the tonic of wildness" (213) may not have included sexuality, but "Higher Laws'" repudiation of physicality, so out of keeping with the rest of *Walden*, seems a sign of weariness, as if when composing this chapter, Thoreau could no longer summon the energy for the vivid life he prized. Indeed, "Higher Laws" ends on precisely that note, replacing wakefulness with abnegation:

Why do you stay here and live this mean moiling life, when a glorious existence is possible for you? Those same stars twinkle over other fields than these.—But how to come out of this condition and actually migrate thither? All that he could think of was to practise some new austerity. (151)

(with Brenda Maxey-Billings)

I

17.

IDLENESS

Walden offers itself as a practical book, but anyone hoping to find a set of immediately operable instructions will be confronted by its contradictory advice. On the one hand, the book's first two chapters and its "Conclusion"—at once Thoreau's most hectoring and inspiring—propose deliberation and effort as the means to a vivid, wide-awake life. In one of *Walden*'s most famous sentences, Thoreau declares, "I know of no more encouraging fact than the unquestionable ability of man to elevate his life by a conscious endeavor" (64). The key word *endeavor* will return near the end:

> I learned this, at least, by my experiment; that if one advances confidently in the direction of his dreams, and endeavors to live the life which he has imagined, he will meet with a success unexpected in common hours. (217)

His repeated insistence that we "put the foundations" under our "castles in the air" (217) casts these parts of *Walden* in the active voice: we can *work* on our lives. "To affect the quality of the day," he concludes, "that is the highest of arts" (65).

This tone appears intermittently throughout *Walden*, with "Higher Laws" offering the most puritanical version: "From exertion come wisdom and purity; from sloth ignorance and sensuality," Thoreau announces, in diction straight out of *Pilgrim's Progress*. "An unclean person is universally a slothful one, one who sits by the stove, whom the sun shines on prostrate, who reposes without being fatigued" (150). And yet this description would also fit Thoreau himself, experiencing one of those "days when idleness was the most attractive and productive industry" (131):

> Sometimes, in a summer morning, having taken my accustomed bath, I sat in my sunny doorway from sunrise till noon, rapt in a revery. (79)

Thoreau admits in *Walden*'s second paragraph that he would not have begun the book "if very particular inquiries had not been made by my townsmen concerning my mode of life, which some would call impertinent" (5). They were right to ask questions. Thoreau had a rare college education and the support of Emerson, the most powerful intellectual in America, but at twenty-eight years old and still without a regular job, he had now taken up solitary residence in a tiny cabin a mile and a half out of town where he was up to God-knows-what. He faced the burden of justifying this apparent shiftlessness, and he intended *Walden*'s opening two chapters, designed as lectures, to make his case. That purpose almost certainly accounts for those chapters' emphasis on strenuous activity (building and planting) and moral enterprise.

Thoreau, of course, had another, far easier, option. If the neighbors got too nosey, he could simply tell the truth: "Look, I'm writing a book as a memorial to my brother, whom you all loved, and I need some uninterrupted time to complete it." In fact, Thoreau spent so much time at Walden writing that his friend Ellery Channing referred to the cabin as "a wooden inkstand." In just twenty-six months, he managed to complete an entire draft of *A Week on the Concord and Merrimack Rivers*, about half of *Walden*, the Ktaadn sections of what would become *The Maine Woods*, and "Civil Disobedience." Given Thoreau's need to explain himself, *Walden*'s almost complete refusal to mention this astonishing literary activity seems perverse, another example of the contrariness Emerson complained about.

Thoreau did, of course, have one very good reason for celebrating the very idleness that bothered his neighbors: doing so enabled him to turn their standard economies upside-down. The italicized words in this passage from "The Ponds," all drawn from business, suggest Thoreau's habit of redefining the most taken-for-granted terms:

> I have *spent* many an hour, when I was younger, floating over [Walden's] surface as the zephyr willed, having pulled my boat to the middle, and lying on my back across the seats, in a summer forenoon, dreaming awake . . . ; days when idleness was the most attractive and *productive industry.* Many a forenoon have I *stolen* away, preferring to *spend* thus the most *valued* part of the day; for I was *rich,* if not in money, in sunny hours and summer days, and I *spent* them lavishly; nor do I regret that I did not *waste* more of them in the workshop or the teacher's desk. (131)

Walden announces a new "economy," in which possessions are burdensome, idleness is productive, labor can be wasteful, and "the cost of a thing is the amount of what I will call life which is required to be exchanged for it, immediately or in the long run" (24). Insisting that he is the most practical man in Concord, Thoreau deploys, for his own ends, all the important economic words—*enterprises, trade, business, capital, accounts, auditing, buying,* and *selling*—renewing our sense of them.

> There are more secrets in my *trade* than in most men's. (15)

> How many mornings, summer and winter, before yet any neighbor was stirring about his *business,* have I been about mine! No doubt, many of my townsmen have met me returning from this *enterprise.* (15)

> So many autumn, ay, and winter days, spent outside the town, trying to hear what was in the wind, to hear and carry it express! I well-nigh sunk all my *capital* in it. (15)

> My *accounts,* which I can swear to have kept faithfully, I have, indeed, never got *audited,* still less accepted, still less *paid and settled.* (16)

> I turned my face more exclusively than ever to the woods, where I was better known. I determined *to go into business* at once. (16)

My purpose in going to Walden Pond was not to live cheaply nor to live dearly there, but *to transact some private business* with the fewest obstacles. (16–17)

I have always endeavored to acquire strict *business* habits; they are indispensable to every man. . . . I have thought that Walden Pond would be a good place for *business* . . . ; it offers advantages which it may not be good policy to divulge . . . (17).

Walden revolves around the economic concept most important to Thoreau, the definition of *value*. What is an object, an experience, an afternoon, a rainfall really worth? Thoreau offers unconventional examples: "It is a surprising and memorable, as well as valuable experience, to be lost in the woods any time" (117). Fishing at night, daydreaming "in my sunny doorway from sunrise till noon" (79), standing in a rainbow's arch—"sheer idleness to my fellow townsmen" (79)—lead to Thoreau's simple bookkeeping entry: "These experiences were very memorable and valuable to me" (120). Of ordinary occupations, he is merely dismissive: "We are made to exaggerate the importance of what work we do" (11).

It's a radical lesson. Emerson confided to his journal that reading Thoreau made him "nervous and wretched," and *Walden* has retained its power to discomfort even the most sympathetic reader. The book may have been ahead of its time. Thoreau's ambivalence about the effort-idleness opposition now seems another version, a transformation or displacement, of something that, because he was a writer, was worrying him even more: the moral imperative, learned from Emerson, to identify a thing's significance versus the sensual pleasure derived from simply describing it. Sharon Cameron has persuasively argued that by ascribing meaning to his experiences, *Walden* compromises the *Journal's* delight in doing without. At times, that compromise seemed to irritate him: "Cut off from . . . AEsop the moral alone at the bottom—would that content you?" (*J*, 28 January 1852) he asks rhetorically. "We need pray for no higher heaven than the pure senses can furnish, a *purely* sensuous life" (*Week*, 382), Thoreau had written in his first book, announcing the radical half of his agenda. The *Journal* offers a lot more in that vein:

Mere facts and names and dates communicate more than we suspect. (*J*, 26 January 1852)

The best thought is not only without somberness—but without morality. . . . The moral aspect of nature is a disease caught of man—a jaundice imported into her. . . . Occasionally we rise above the necessity of virtue into an unchangeable morning light—in which we have not to choose in a dilemma between right and wrong—but simply to live right on and breathe the circumambient air. (*J*, 1 August 1841)

I begin to see . . . objects only when I leave off understanding them. (*J*, 14 February 1851)

"Description," Roland Barthes once observed, "has its spiritual equivalent in contemplation." In the mid-nineteenth century, however, this repudiation of meaning could only have seemed scandalous, precisely the term Barthes used to describe the same process, which he associated with "bliss" or "pleasure." The relevant passage, from *The Pleasure of the Text,* could be a description of what we now call "Thoreau":

It is a drift, something both revolutionary and asocial, and it cannot be taken over by any collectivity, and mentality, any ideolect. . . . It is . . . scandalous: not because it is immoral but because it is *atopic.*

In the same book, while describing another writer's journals, Barthes identifies the dilemma confronting Thoreau:

Why do some people, including myself, enjoy in certain novels, biographies, and historical works the representation of the "daily life" of an epoch, of a character? Why this curiosity about petty details: schedules, habits, meals, lodging, clothing, etc.?

Thus, impossible to imagine a more tenuous, a more insignificant notation than that of "today's weather" (or yesterday's); and yet, the other day, reading, trying to read Amiel, irritation that the well-meaning editor (another person foreclosing pleasure) had seen fit to omit from this Journal the everyday details, what the weather was like on the shores of Lake Geneva, and retain only insipid moral musing: yet it is this weather that has not aged, not Amiel's philosophy.

"What the weather was like"—it's an exact description of what interested Thoreau: "In a journal," he wrote to himself, "it is important in a few words to describe the weather, or character of the day, as it affects our feelings. That which was so important at the time cannot be unimportant to remember" (*J*, 5 February 1855). An 1841 journal entry even exactly anticipates Barthes's resistance to Amiel's "insipid moral musing":

> In reading a work on agriculture, I skip the author's moral reflections . . . to come at the profitable level of what he has to say. There is no science in men's religion; it does not teach me so much as the report of the committee on swine. My author shows that he has dealt in corn and turnips and can worship God with the hoe and spade, but spare me the morality. (*J*, 1 April 1841)

Barthes would eventually recognize the object of this longing: photography. With its amoral objectivity, the camera simply *records*, thereby offering an escape from language's inevitable judgments. In an 1851 journal entry, Thoreau's diction inadvertently suggests that he had begun to grasp this point:

> It would be a truer discipline for the writer to take the least film of thought that floats in the twilight sky of his mind for his theme, about which he has scarcely one idea (that would be teaching his ideas how to shoot). (*J*, 25 December 1851)

One historian cites the early photographer Fox Talbot's surprise at this effect:

> And that was just the trouble: fascinating irrelevancy. "Sometimes inscriptions and dates are found upon buildings, or printed placards most irrelevant, are discovered upon their walls: sometimes a distant sundial is seen, and upon it—unconsciously recorded—the hour of the day at which the view was taken."

One of *Walden*'s central difficulties involves Thoreau's willingness to reopen a basic literary question: what counts as relevance? As the book scatters its incidental records and descriptions, its meticulous accounts of the pond's depths and the winter freezes, what Stanley Cavell calls "its drones of fact," the reader begins to experience the equivalent of a photograph's "fascinating irrelevancy" and also, perhaps, Fox Talbot's fear "that the instrument was only partially under control, recording disinterestedly in despite of its operator's intentions." After "Economy" and "Where I Lived and What I Lived For," Thoreau's versions of a conventional argument, *Walden* sometimes seems to lose its way, as if its author has set in motion something—a habit of attention, a resistance to conventional proprieties, a love of the commonplace—that begins to operate on its own. "Give me a sentence which no intelligence can understand" (*Week,* 151), Thoreau wrote at Walden. That sentence would be a photograph.

Barthes consistently associated the production of meaning with work. Details without either informational or symbolic value—in semiotic terms, signifiers without signifieds—were "a luxury," "increasing the cost of narrative information," a precise diagnosis of *Walden*'s effect on most readers. Barthes found such details in fiction (an old piano, a barometer), where their irrelevance guaranteed "the reality effect." He also discovered them in film stills (a kerchief's fall across a woman's forehead, a woman's chignon), where they "disturb" and "sterilize" the possibility of straightforward meaning, becoming "the epitome of counter-narrative," "an unheard-of script, counter-logical and yet 'true.'" These "third meanings," as Barthes paradoxically named them, represent a kind of suspension, when the engine of significance *idles.*

The significance-description opposition had already appeared in the essays of the cinema's most important theoretician, André Bazin. In "The Ontology of the Photographic Image" (1945) and "The Evolution of the Language of Cinema" (1950, 1952, 1955), Bazin had argued that the two most prestigious schools of filmmaking (Soviet montage and German expressionism) had undermined photography's most radical feature, its ability to provide an objective depiction of reality. By imposing meaning on their photographed material, these schools' abstracting montages and grotesque mise-en-scènes had turned the cinema into just another form of writing. In their place, Bazin called for "a form of self-effacement before reality" that would let the world reveal itself. He admired films like *The Bicycle Thieves*, whose "events are not necessarily signs of something[;] . . . they all carry their own weight[,] . . . that ambiguity that characterizes any fact."

Thoreau had been there before him. "Express" a fact, he counseled, "without expressing yourself." Thoreau's journals amount to cinematic rushes, the record of an idling, alert sensibility recording with the automatism of a camera (a word that never appears in *Walden*). In a 9 April 1841 journal entry, he anticipates Bazin's credo: "How much virtue there is in simply seeing!" On 27 February of the same year, Thoreau describes a bright winter day: "Life looks . . . fair at this moment[,] . . . so washed in light, so untried. . . . All its flags are flowing. . . . this pure, unwiped hour." A film scene anticipating a story? A film scene not needing a story? A world "washed" of what? Of imposed meaning?

Many of *Walden*'s interior passages seem content merely to record, as Thoreau anticipates Christopher Isherwood's famous opening sentence, "I am a camera":

> Sometimes, in a summer morning, having taken my accustomed
> bath, I sat in my sunny doorway from sunrise until noon, rapt in
> a revery, amidst the pines and hickories and sumachs, in undis-
> turbed solitude and stillness, while the birds sang around or flitted
> noiseless through the house, until by the sun falling in at my west
> window, or the noise of some traveler's wagon on the distant high-
> way, I was reminded of the lapse of time. (79)

Thoreau, however, remained wary of his own penchant for idleness, drift, and mere description. His books resemble completed films—edited, composed, arranged into meaning. Even in his journal, Thoreau often becomes something like Amiel, making morals everywhere, or like an early photographer, convinced that the simple record of things cannot possibly count as "art" without the tendentiousness of special effects (gauze, soft focus, etc.)—photography's moralizing. In this context, this ambivalent *Walden* passage seems freshly pertinent:

> One day, when my axe had come off and I had cut a green hickory
> for a wedge, driving it with a stone, and had placed the whole to

soak in a pond hole in order to swell the wood, I saw a striped snake run into the water, and he lay on the bottom, apparently without inconvenience, as long as I stayed there, or more than a quarter of an hour, perhaps because he had not yet fairly come out of the torpid state. It appeared to me that for a like reason men remain in their low and primitive condition; but if they should feel the influence of the spring of springs arousing them, they would of necessity rise to a higher and more ethereal life. I had previously seen the snakes in frosty mornings in my path with portions of their bodies still numb and inflexible, waiting for the sun to thaw them. On the 1st of April it rained and melted the ice, and in the early part of the day, which was very foggy, I heard a stray goose groping about over the pond and cackling as if lost, or like the spirit of the fog.

Note how the last sentence (what the weather was like on the shores of Walden Pond) slips free from the smothering lesson offered before. Does the lesson amount to a kind of cinematic montage that hijacks the details of a particular day for an imposed purpose? If so, why does Thoreau not end the passage there? Does the last sentence represent Thoreau's own longing for the photography he never mentions? For the sheer stuff of everyday life, freed from the obligation to mean? For idleness?

(with Hanif Ali and Carly Roach)

18.

4 JULY 1845

When first I took up my abode in the woods, that is began to
spend my nights as well as my days there, which, by accident, was
on Independence Day, or the fourth of July 1845, my house was
not finished for winter. (61)

At least since Stanley Cavell's influential *The Senses of Walden*
(1972), we have assumed that Thoreau's choice to move to the woods
on the Fourth of July was no "accident." Calling his venture an
"experiment," Thoreau was, in Cavell's terms, reenacting the original settlement of America, a continent itself accidently discovered,
whose betrayed promise Thoreau now took on himself to redeem.
It's a compelling argument, one that would connect *Walden* to *The
Great Gatsby*'s rapt conclusion:

Most of the big shore places were closed now and there were
hardly any lights except the shadowy, moving glow of a ferryboat
across the Sound. And as the moon rose higher the inessential
houses began to melt away until gradually I became aware of
the old island here that flowered once for Dutch sailors' eyes—a
fresh, green breast of the new world. Its vanished trees, the trees
that had made way for Gatsby's house, had once pandered in
whispers to the last and greatest of all human dreams; for a tran-
sitory enchanted moment man must have held his breath in the
presence of this continent, compelled into an aesthetic contemplation he neither understood nor desired, face to face for the

last time in history with something commensurate to his capacity for wonder.

Although Thoreau was, in some ways, simply squatting, barely a mile and a half from his family's house, on Emerson's land, *Walden* represents his venture as a heroic isolation, an exploration designed to get things right at last: "I went to the woods because I wished to live deliberately," he declares, "to front only the essential facts of life, and see if I could not learn what it had to teach (65). Thoreau's "capacity for wonder" at his discovery often equals Fitzgerald's:

> Where I lived was a far off as many a region viewed nightly by astronomers. . . . I discovered that my house actually had its site in such a withdrawn, but forever new and unprofaned, part of the universe. . . . I was really there, or at least at an equal remoteness from the life which I had left behind, dwindled and twinkling with as fine a ray to my nearest neighbor, and to be seen only in moonless nights by him. (63)

"We are the subjects of an experiment" (94), Thoreau writes, speaking perhaps for all Americans, and implicitly acknowledging the Fourth of July's symbolic significance. In one of the *Week*'s most urgent passages, he had already appropriated the frontier metaphor to dramatize his own existential project:

> The frontiers are not east or west, north or south, but wherever a man *fronts* a fact, though that fact be his neighbor, there is an unsettled wilderness between him and Canada, between him and the setting sun, or, further still, between him and *it*. Let him build himself a log-house with the bark on where he is, *fronting* IT, and wage there an Old French war for seven or seventy years, with Indians and Rangers, or whatever else may come between him and the reality, and save his scalp if he can (*Week*, 304).

There are signs, however, that Thoreau cared little about the collective activity called "America." From 1837 to 1860, not a single Fourth of July journal entry mentions the national holiday. He is too busy recording the landscape and the weather:

July 4, 1853: The cotton-grass at Beck Stow's. Is it different from the early one? High blueberries begin.

July 4, 1854: A sultry night the last; bear no covering; all windows open. . . . A very hot day.

July 4, 1860: Gentle rain in the night (last). . . . Standing on J. P. Brown's land, south side, I observed his rich and luxuriant uncut grass-lands northward, now waving under the easterly wind. . . . None of his fields is cut yet.

Walden makes explicit his indifference to public memorials. Describing the "martial strains" of a military band, honoring either Independence Day or the Concord Battle, he comments sarcastically, "This was one of the *great* days," before returning to his own concerns, "though the sky had from my clearing only the same everlastingly great look that it wears daily, and I saw no difference in it" (111). Thoreau, in other words, is always willing to exploit the symbolic implications of his adventure, but he is less concerned with America than with, as he puts it, "faithfully minding my business" (16). "Wherever I sat, there I might live," he announces, in an unabashed acknowledgment of solipsism, "and the landscape radiated from me accordingly" (58).

The opening salvo of "Economy" makes no attempt to conceal Thoreau's contempt for "Doing-good," "one of the professions which are full" (53). "But all this is very selfish, I have heard some of my townsmen say," he remarks, introducing an attack on philanthropy that anticipates Nietzsche's diagnosis of its selfishness: we praise another for sacrificing his or her interests because it benefits *us*. Thoreau counsels self-culture: instead of doing good, "I should say rather, Set about being good" (53).

> If, then, we would indeed restore mankind . . . let us first be as simple and well as Nature ourselves, dispel the clouds which hang over our own brows, and take up a little life into our pores. Do not stay to be an overseer of the poor, but endeavor to become one of the worthies of the world. (57)

Joel Porte once observed that "*Walden* is notoriously poor as a blueprint for improving society. (Thoreau's wry humor allowed him to perpetrate *that* joke.) The book is really a description of Thoreau's dream, to a large extent realized, of perfected self-indulgence and self-possession."

We cannot, however, easily dismiss Cavell's emphasis on the Fourth of July: if Jay Gatz's desire for Daisy Buchanan can evoke the American Dream, then certainly Thoreau's provocative retreat to Walden can reimagine American possibilities. A man living alone in the woods, in a cabin built with his own hands, beside a small farm he has planted—these elements, as Thoreau well knew, are inevitably allegorical. They are parts of a sustained dramatic gesture, and the Fourth of July is crucial to it.

K

19.

KITTLYBENDERS

It affords me no satisfaction to commence to spring an arch before
I have got a solid foundation. Let us not play at kittlybenders.
There is a solid bottom every where. (222)

In the third Norton critical edition of *Walden,* William Rossi's
footnote defines *kittlybenders* as "a game in which children attempt
to run or skate on thin ice without breaking it" (222), but the word
would probably be entirely forgotten if Thoreau had not mentioned
it as something *not* to play. Since Thoreau enjoyed skating, covering,
according to Richardson (334), as much as thirty miles at a stretch
and reaching fourteen miles an hour, why does he reject kittlybenders? Thoreau's characteristic strategy in *Walden* involves using
architectural and spatial vocabulary to represent thinking and living. Thus, kittlybenders' literal danger serves as a metaphor for the
hazards of a life without foundations, an argument without grounds.
"There is a solid bottom everywhere," Thoreau reminds us, in a figure that recurs in *Walden:*

I have thought that Walden Pond would be a good place for business . . . ; it offers advantages which it may not be a good policy to
divulge; it is a good port and a good foundation. No Neva marshes
to be filled; though you must every where build on piles of your
own driving. (17–18)

Let us settle ourselves, and work and wedge our feet downward through the mud and slush of opinion, and prejudice, and tradition, and delusion, and appearance . . . till we come to a hard bottom and rocks in place, which we can call *reality,* and say, This is, and no mistake. (70)

If you have built castles in the air, your work need not be lost; that is where they should be. Now put the foundations under them. (217)

In "The Pond in Winter," Thoreau goes to great lengths to disprove the local myths of Walden's bottomlessness, characteristically using the literal sense to remark that these stories "certainly had no foundation for themselves" (191). Thoreau may have borrowed this stylistic habit from Emerson, who could even deploy architectural terms to criticize his own arguments' lack of specifics: "I found that when I had finished my new lecture that it was a very good house," he once confided to his journal, "only the architect had unfortunately omitted the stairs."

The image of children playing kittlybenders evokes the closely related expression, "to skate on thin ice," whose earliest use, if not invention, Eric Partridge's *A Dictionary of Clichés* attributes to Emerson himself. "In skating over thin ice," Emerson wrote circa 1860, "our safety is in our speed." Here, Emerson seems more practical than Thoreau, modifying *Walden*'s warning to read something like, "Let us not play at kittlybenders *slowly.*" Thoreau, of course, had ample experience with thin ice. *Walden*'s thick descriptions of the pond's cover typically favor the days of first freeze and first melting, precisely the moments of the ice's greatest thinness. "The first ice is especially interesting and perfect," "House-Warming" suggests: "You can lie at your length on ice only an inch thick, like a skater insect on the surface of the water, and study the bottom at your leisure, only two or three inches distant, like a picture behind a glass" (166). In "Spring," Thoreau is equally alert to Walden's breaking up: "The ice in the pond at length begins to be honey-combed, and I can set my heel in it as I walk" (203).

But as Emerson observed, kittlybenders depends on *speed,* and to the extent that Thoreau sees the game as a metaphor for writing and living, he rejects it. For despite Thoreau's quickness as a skater, as a writer he was not fast. His twenty-six-month stay at Walden did prove enormously productive: he completed a full draft of *A Week on the Concord and Merrimack Rivers,* the first chapters of *Walden,* "Civil Disobedience," the essay on Thomas Carlyle, and parts of what would become *The Maine Woods.* After that period, however, his pace slowed, and the completed *Walden* did not appear for seven years. The kittlybenders metaphor suggests the reason. Since Thoreau's journal, begun in 1837, runs to nearly two million words (for years, he wrote in it almost every day), we clearly cannot diagnose him with anything like a writer's block. But for all the ready inspiration pouring into his daily writing, Thoreau assumed that his lectures, published essays, and books demanded more scaffolding. Richardson frequently uses the phrase "worked up" to describe the passage from journal to essay (e.g., "Thoreau worked up the moonlight material [from his journals] into a lecture"), and those words suggest a slow, deliberate structuring of an argument rather than a quick glide. When *Walden* seems boring, it is usually because the machinery is showing.

Thoreau was aware of the problem. In an 1841 journal entry, he accurately described his own composition method:

> From all points of the compass, from the earth beneath and the heavens above, have come these inspirations and been entered duly in the order of their arrival in the journal. Thereafter, when the time arrived, they are winnowed into lectures, and again, in due time, from lectures into essays. (*J,* summer 1845)

By 27 January 1852, he had begun to question this procedure:

> I do not know but thoughts written down thus in a journal might be printed in the same form with greater advantage—than if the related ones were brought together into separate essays. They are now allied to life—& are seen by the reader not to be far-fetched. (*J,* 27 January 1852)

By mistrusting the speed on which kittlybenders depended, Thoreau had committed himself to writing strategies that always ran the risk of seeming "far-fetched"—the organization of the *Week* according to the days of the week, Walden according to the seasons of a single year. Of his contemporaries, Margaret Fuller seems the first to have intuited the problem with Thoreau's working procedure. She rejected a submission to the Dial with this diagnosis:

> Last night's second reading only confirms my impression from the first. The essay is rich in thoughts, and I should be pained not to meet it again. But then, the thoughts seem to me so out of their natural order that I cannot read it through without pain. I never once felt myself in a stream of thought, but seem to hear the grating tools on the mosaic.

In fact, all of Thoreau's "books" are mosaics, constructed out of journal entries written over a period of years, what Andrew Delbanco has called "modular blocks that can be placed in new relations with others composed in entirely discrete moods and moments." Although Thoreau increasingly preferred the spontaneity of journal writing, he did not trust it as the proper form for a book. Perhaps he was right. Although Michel Serres once observed that "the most elegant demonstration is always the shortest one," Thoreau was willing to sacrifice elegance for persuasion. He intended Walden to be an argument that would explain why, in Rilke's phrase, "you must change your life." Making that argument took time. With a similar ambition, Wittgenstein settled on the opposite procedure: "What he did," David Pears reports, "was to write in these notebooks day by day, and then he made selections winnowing out a lot of materials, and in some case omitting the details of his arguments" (emphasis added), thereby making his work opaque but vivid. But can a philosopher proposing something as radical as Walden play at kittlybenders, skate quickly over thin ice? Nietzsche thought so:

> For I approach deep problems like cold baths: quickly into them and quickly out again. That one does not get to the depths that way, not deep enough down, is the superstition of those afraid of the water, the enemies of cold water; they speak without experience. The freezing cold makes one swift.
>   And to ask this incidentally: does a matter necessarily remain ununderstood and unfathomed merely because it has been

touched only in flight, glanced at, in a flash? Is it absolutely imperative that one settles down on it?

Although Thoreau enacted Nietzsche's metaphor by taking morning baths in the pond's cold water ("a religious exercise, and one of the best things which I did" [63]), he took up residence at Walden to work on a question: "I went to the woods because I wished to live deliberately, to front only the essential facts of life, and see if I could not learn what it had to teach" (65). He refused to work quickly. For twenty six months, he "settled down" to that question, in Nietzsche's phrase, looking for his argument's foundation, refusing to play kittlybenders:

Let us settle ourselves, and work and wedge our feet downward
. . . till we come to a hard bottom and rocks in place, which we can
call *reality,* and say, This is, and no mistake." (70)
(with Charles Meyer)

L

20.

LEAVING WALDEN

Walden's celebration of Thoreau's glorious twenty-six months in the woods leaves almost all of its readers with a stark question: why did he choose to leave? The book's "Conclusion," of course, offers one explanation, but its laconic offhandness has never proved very satisfying:

> I left the woods for as good a reason as I went there. Perhaps it seemed to me that I had several more lives to live, and could not spare any more time for that one. (217)

"I left the woods for as good a reason as I went there"—what could that sentence mean? In "Where I Lived and What I Lived For," Thoreau had already spelled out his reason for *going to* the pond: "I went to the woods because I wished to live deliberately, to front only the essential facts of life, and see if I could not learn what it had to teach" (65). With its senses of care, consideration, and unhurriedness, *deliberately* does a lot of work in that passage, endowing Thoreau's move to the woods with the aura of an existential choice. As he set about finishing *Walden*, Thoreau had certainly come to recognize that choice as the decisive one of his life, the one that had given him the most immediate happiness and prompted the writing that would establish his reputation.

That decision had not been hasty. Thoreau had been thinking for some time about withdrawing from Concord society and his parents' house, if only for some privacy (his mother took in borders).

He wanted no part of communal experiments like Brook Farm. He began to settle on Walden Pond, familiar to him since childhood, but even after Emerson's offer of the land he had purchased in the fall of 1844, the actual move required nearly four full months of preparation, devoted mainly to clearing the ground and building the cabin. Thus, by implying that his sudden decision *to leave* the woods simply matched the original impulse to go there, Thoreau is being disingenuous. While his departure seems as abrupt as the sentences that announce it ("Thus was my first year's life in the woods completed; and the second year was similar to it. I finally left Walden September 6th, 1847" [214]), the arrival had been anything but.

Even *Walden*'s vague explanation for his departure seems more decisive than the corresponding *Journal* entry, where the sudden abandonment of his hard-won solitude seems unintelligible even to Thoreau himself:

> But Why I changed—? Why I left the woods? I do not think I can tell. I have often wished myself back—I do not know any better how I ever came to go there—. Perhaps it is none of my business— even if it is yours. Perhaps I wanted a change—There was a little stagnation it may be—about 2 o'clock in the afternoon the world's axle—creaked as if it needed greasing—as if the oxen labored—& could hardly get their load over the ridge of the day—Perhaps if I lived there much longer I might live there forever—One would think twice before he accepted heaven on such terms. (*J*, 22 January 1852)

By suppressing the crucial phrase, "I have often wished myself back," Thoreau was simply continuing his practice of removing from *Walden*'s final version any hints of self-doubt or melancholy. In another elided passage, he made explicit this working procedure: "I will tell him [the reader] this secret, if he will not abuse my confidence—I put the best face on the matter." But wouldn't "the best face on the matter" of his departure have simply been to mention its immediate cause, a request from the Emersons that Thoreau resume living in their house while Ralph was lecturing in Europe?

During the seven years between his leaving the woods and *Walden*'s appearance, while he worked over its multiple drafts,

Thoreau had certainly begun to acknowledge that he had passed the high-water mark of his life. In 1851, he confided to his journal:

> Methinks my present experience is nothing; my past experience is all in all, I think that no experience which I have today comes up to, or is comparable with, the experiences of my boyhood. . . . Formerly, methought, nature developed as I developed, and grew up with me. My life was ecstasy. In youth, before I lost any of my senses, I can remember that I was all alive. (*J*, 16 July 1851)

In *Walden*, this kind of regret appears only between the cracks. As Thoreau announces in the book's epigraph, in a sentence his second chapter repeats, "I do not propose to write an ode to dejection, but to brag as lustily as chanticleer in the morning" (5, 60–61). We can sense that dejection, however, in the tense of an apparently casual phrase, "In Arcadia, when I was there" (42).

Thus, while it is tempting to attribute Thoreau's departure from his cabin to his having finished the writing he had gone there to do—especially the *Week,* his brother's memorial, which had been hanging fire for three years—the *Journal* entries and *Walden* itself (which never mentions writing) make clear that he always thought of his venture as more than just an artist's workshop. The *Journal*'s teeming abundance indicates that Thoreau could write anywhere, although he may have needed sustained solitude to achieve the longer forms requiring architectural structure. But the intermittent excitement felt by *Walden*'s reader results from the sense that Thoreau was playing for the highest possible stakes. "My purpose," he writes, "was to transact some private business" (16–17), and that business was learning how to live.

Having left the woods, Thoreau seemed to discover that he could not recreate the same experience elsewhere. Fishing at night (121), getting lost in the woods (117–18), standing in the middle of the frozen pond (124), feeling "a gentle rain in August" (62), hearing the echo of bells ring across a hillside (87), dazzled by a rainbow's arch that scattered its colors over the grass (138), or simply recording "This is a delicious evening" (90)—Thoreau was discovering *a mood* that taught him the crucial lesson: "We should be blessed if we lived in the present always and took advantage of every accident that befell us" (211). In effect, he had anticipated Heidegger's proposition—based on the coincidence that the German word for "mood" (*Stimmung*) also means a musical "pitch" or "tuning"—that far from being something trivial, a mood *disposes* us to the world in a particular way. In Heidegger's example, a peaceful evening's stroll down an empty alley gets transformed by the sudden arrival of fear. Heidegger thought that "moods assail us" (*überfallen*) and that our very inability to control them enables us "to encounter something that matters to us." A prevailing mood becomes "like an atmosphere in which we at first immerse ourselves . . . and which then attunes us through and through."

Thoreau understood this lesson. In "Solitude," he describes "a slight insanity in my mood," healed by "a gentle rain" that revealed Nature's beneficence, "like an atmosphere sustaining me" (92). *Walden* is a record of his repeated efforts to "tune" his moods to match the pitch of the world. To a large extent, that adjustment involved learning to "[take] advantage of every accident" that happened to him. It also required an abandonment of his own insistence that "all nature will *fable*, and every natural phenomenon be a myth" (*J*, 10 May 1853). *Walden* demonstrates the means for achieving that mood: the gradual replacement of significance with description. By the end of the book's penultimate chapter, Thoreau can announce this new disposition:

> We need the tonic of wildness. . . . At the same time that we are earnest to explore and learn all things, we require that all things be mysterious and unexplorable, that land and sea be infinitely wild, unsurveyed and unfathomed by us because unfathomable. . . . We need to witness our own limits transgressed, and some life pasturing freely where we never wander. (213)

Unlike Heidegger, however, Thoreau believed that he could deliberately (that word again) achieve a particular mood: "I know of no more encouraging fact than the unquestionable ability of man to elevate his life by a conscious endeavor" (64), he observes in "Where I Lived and What I Lived For." With its careful accounts of house building, planting, reading, walks, morning idylls, measurements, and factual cataloguing, *Walden* amounts to a detailed set of instructions about how to get in tune with the world. To the extent that he had misplaced that mood after leaving the woods, Thoreau was compiling those instructions for himself.

M

21.

MOLTING

Our moulting season, like that of the fowls, must be a crisis in our lives. The loon retires to solitary ponds to spend it. Thus also the snake casts its slough, and the caterpillar its wormy coat, by an internal industry and expansion. (19)

The molting process Thoreau describes strikingly resembles his own Walden experiment: he retires to the pond to protect himself from public scrutiny of his radical social opinions and vocational diffidence. The image of the awkward molting fowl becomes a metaphor for Thoreau's own transformation. Like the bird, whose plumage becomes irregular, Thoreau's thoughts and feelings about his enterprise vacillated: indeed, his public attitudes, recorded in *Walden*, often contradict the private ones, confided to his journal, even when written concurrently. "I put the best face on the matter," he admitted. Thoreau describes his own molting as a linear progression that begins with a revelation (the virtues of austerity), proceeds with a transformative journey (the retreat to the pond), and ends with the emergence of a new man, who, having cast off everything unnecessary, "can, like the old philosopher, walk out the gate empty-handed without anxiety" (20).

Although molting is a natural process, inescapable for the species that experience it, Thoreau's own "molting" is "deliberate," the word he uses to describe his project: "I went to the woods because I wished to live deliberately" (65). Indeed, this purposefulness enables his celebration of the "encouraging fact . . . the unquestionable ability of a man to elevate his life by a conscious endeavor" (64). By describing "our moulting season" as "a crisis in our lives," Thoreau evokes Emerson's 1838 "Literary Ethics," a lecture delivered to Dartmouth College's graduating seniors. Its conclusion represents Emerson at his most inspiring:

> Gentlemen, I have ventured to offer you these considerations upon the scholar's place, and hope, because I thought, that, standing, as many of you now do, on the threshold of the College, girt and ready to go and assume tasks, public and private, in your country, you would not be sorry to be admonished of those primary duties of the intellect, whereof you will seldom hear from the lips of your new companions. You will hear every day the maxims of a low prudence. You will hear, that the first duty is to get land and money, place and name. "What is this Truth you seek? what is this Beauty?" men will ask, with derision. If, nevertheless, God have called any of you to explore truth and beauty, be bold, be firm, be true. When you shall say, "As others do, so will I: I renounce, I am sorry for it, my early visions; I must eat the good of the land, and let learning and romantic expectations go, until a more convenient season";—then dies the man in you; then once more perish the buds of art, and poetry, and science, as they have died already in a thousand thousand men. *The hour of that choice is the crisis of your history* [emphasis added]; and see that you hold yourself fast by the intellect. . . . Be content with a little light, so it be your own. Explore, and explore. Be neither chided nor flattered out of your position of perpetual inquiry. . . . Make yourself necessary to the world.

The crisis Emerson describes, the transition from school into adult life, is as unavoidable as a bird's molting, a natural product of the maturation season. Thoreau, however, had *provoked* his own crisis in order to force himself to become a new man. By describing this action as "molting," he merely continues his habit of using natural metaphors for existential purposes. Nevertheless, he had so thoroughly absorbed Emerson's lesson that his mentor's refusal to acknowledge *Walden*, even in his own journal, remains a mystery. Passages in Emerson's eulogy for Thoreau often recall the Dartmouth address:

At this time, a strong and healthy youth fresh from college, whilst all his companions were choosing their professions, or eager to begin some lucrative employment, it was inevitable that his thoughts should be exercises on the same question, and it required rare decision to refuse all accustomed paths, and keep his solitary freedom at the cost of disappointing the natural expectations of his family and friends. . . . But Thoreau never faltered. He was a born protestant. He declined to give up his large ambition of knowledge and action for any narrow craft or profession, aiming at a much more comprehensive calling, the art of living well.

And yet, Emerson would conclude that Thoreau "had no ambition." "Hold yourself fast by the intellect." "Be content with a little light, so be it your own." "Explore, and explore." "Make yourself necessary to the world." These had been Emerson's counsels, his advice to those facing "the crisis of your history." Did any of Emerson's readers ever put those words into practice more conscientiously, more rigorously, more consistently than Thoreau?

(with Alex Washington)

22.

NAME

Although *Walden* has always been attributed to Henry David Thoreau, its author was actually christened David Henry Thoreau. At some point after college, Thoreau simply reversed the order of his first two names, perhaps to accommodate his parents' habit of calling him Henry, perhaps as an early exercise in self-determination. This step, which accepts the given as an occasion for rearrangement, provides the key to *Walden*.

Walden's reputation as a near-sacred text often provokes disappointment in its readers. If we expect the book to reveal the meaning of life, we may feel let down by its lessons, which, when paraphrased and stripped of Thoreau's elevated prose, can seem platitudinous: life is what you make of it! Reduce your needs, and you can work less! Nature is beautiful! In fact, however, *Walden* proposes that the secret to living well depends not on the discovery of some hidden truth but rather on rearranging what already lies before us. Thoreau doesn't propose to reinvent civilization from scratch; he simply reorders its existing components. This process, outlined in "Economy," involves the promotion of fundamental needs over inessential luxuries, reversing the unnatural order he detects in his neighbors' lives. As early as 1837, in his Harvard commencement address ("The Commercial Spirit"), Thoreau had revealed his readiness to shake up even a biblical dispensation: "The order of things should be somewhat reversed," he had announced. "The seventh day should be man's day of toil, wherein to earn his living by the sweat of his brow; and the other six his Sabbath of the affections and the soul." In *Walden,* the ratio of leisure to work has increased: "I found that by working about six weeks in a year, I could meet all the expenses of living" (50). Suggesting the continuity of his ideas, Thoreau's conclusion uses the language of his Harvard speech: "It is not necessary that a man should earn his living by the sweat of his brow, unless he sweats easier than I do" (52).

This faith in rearrangement explains *Walden*'s celebration of getting lost: it loosens the hold of habitual perception, typically regarded by Thoreau as deadening. Thus, his narrative of a night return to his cabin ("It is darker in the woods, even in common nights, than most suppose" [117]) results in a lesson about the advantages of disorientation:

> It is a surprising and memorable, as well as valuable experience, to be lost in the woods at any time. Often in a snow storm, even by day, one will come out upon a well-known road and yet find it impossible to tell which way leads to the village. Though he knows that he has travelled it a thousand times, he cannot recognize a feature in it, but it is as strange to him as if it were a road in Siberia. . . . [N]ot till we are completely lost, or turned around . . . do we appreciate the vastness and strangeness of Nature. . . . Not till we are lost, in other words, not till we have lost the world, do we begin to find ourselves, and realize where we are and the infinite extent of our relations. (117–18)

Wittgenstein's philosophical method would repeat Thoreau's move: "Problems are solved," he observed, "not by reporting new experience, but by arranging what we have always known." Wittgenstein compared this activity to rearranging books on a shelf, observing that "the onlooker who doesn't know the difficulty of the task might well think . . . that nothing at all has been achieved.— The difficulty in philosophy is to say no more than we know." The kinds of hopes aroused by *Walden* for some previously unimagined revelation inhibit our ability to appreciate Thoreau's lesson. "One of the greatest hindrances to philosophy," Wittgenstein insisted, "is the expectation of new, unheard of discoveries." "We have only to put together in the right way what we *know*, without adding anything, and the satisfaction we are trying to get from explanation comes of itself." "Nature puts no questions and answers none" (189), Thoreau concludes. "Heaven is under our feet as well as over our heads" (190). Nothing important is hidden; we simply have to see what lies all around us:

> The change from storm and winter to serene and mild weather, from dark and sluggish hours to bright and elastic ones, is a memorable crisis which all things proclaim. It is seemingly instantaneous at last. Suddenly an influx of light filled my house, though the evening was at hand and the clouds of winter still overhung it, and the eaves were dripping with sleety rain. I looked out the window, and lo! where yesterday was cold gray ice there lay the transparent pond already calm and full of hope as on a summer evening. (209)

This approach seems easy enough: "Since everything lies open to view there is nothing to explain." Taken as an instruction, Wittgenstein's dictum would seem to endorse *Walden*'s meticulous descriptions of Thoreau's personal economy, the seasons' accumulating momentum, the natural phenomena and wildlife he observed in the woods. But lost in *Walden*'s interior chapters, a reader can begin to sense the problem Wittgenstein acknowledged with his own descriptive method: "What we say will be easy, but to know why we say it will be very difficult." Thoreau's meticulous accounts of the pond's first freezes, of a solitary loon's frolicking, of his own tracks made in the snow—such typical passages are not hard to understand, but we may find ourselves asking: Why am I being told these things? If, as Wittgenstein diagnosed, "the aspects of things that are most important for us are hidden because of their simplicity and familiarity," simply showing those things in a new light, by rearranging them, will have an instructive effect. Doing so requires method.

Wittgenstein's own preferred method was the "language game," an imaginary situation whose constraints expose language's workings. How, for example, would a tribe of builders with only four words—"Block!" "Pillar!" "Slab!" and "Beam!"—teach a child its language? How does the child learn that "Slab!" means "Bring that slab here to me" and not, "Place that slab on top of the other one"? How can we decide when the child has mastered the builders' language?

"It disperses the fog," Wittgenstein argued, "to study the phenomena of language in primitive kinds of applications in which one can command a clear view of the aim and functioning of the words."

Thoreau had intuited this approach: "It would be some advantage to live a primitive and frontier life, though in the midst of an outward civilization, if only to learn what are the gross necessaries of life and what methods have been taken to obtain them" (11). By restricting himself to solitude, to a cabin and food of his own making, to his own observations of the world around him, Thoreau at Walden was enacting a "language game" of his own invention. If Wittgenstein's games enable us to see how we learn to use a word, Thoreau's offers to teach us how he learned to live a life.

(with Adam Nikolaidis)

23

NUMBERS

- 2,000: population of Concord during Thoreau's stay at the pond
- 2 years, 2 months, 2 days: length of Thoreau's stay at Walden (before deducting a month spent at home while his cabin was being winterproofed and his two-week Maine trip)
- 1.3 miles: distance from Thoreau's cabin to Emerson's house
- 28–36: Thoreau's age during *Walden*'s composition
- 550 yards: distance from Thoreau's cabin to the Fitchburg railroad line
- 204 feet: distance from Thoreau's cabin to Walden Pond
- 612 acres: size of Walden Pond
- 31: tools Thoreau used at Walden
- over 3,000: uses of first-person pronoun in *Walden*
- less than half a mile: distance from Thoreau's cabin to Irish railroad laborers' huts
- 10' x 15': size of Thoreau's cabin
- 30: people that could fit in the cabin without removing the furniture
- almost 7 miles: total length of Thoreau's bean rows
- over 700: references to animals in *Walden*
- 6: languages Thoreau could read fluently (English, Latin, Greek, French, German, Italian)
- 25: Harvard faculty members when Thoreau was a student
- over $1 million: 1988 sale price of Thoreau family house

O

24.

OBSCURITY

"I do not suppose that I have attained to obscurity" (218), Thoreau concludes, in a phrase so off-handed, so modest, so *good natured* that it conceals, in a manner absolutely characteristic of his writing, a startling complexity. For by trailing connotations of deliberate striving, "attained" converts *obscurity* from a "fatal flaw" into a longed-for goal, and abruptly Thoreau's apparently innocent words align with his uncompromising ones: "Give me a sentence which no intelligence can understand" (*Week*, 151). Since all communication operates under the threat of illegibility, which most rhetoric exists to forestall, why would Thoreau wish to court obscurity, with its attendant responses "I don't understand," "I don't follow you, "I don't see"?

This move has been recognizable to us at least since the French symbolists' attempt to make poetry resemble music, to rid it of any overt "subject matter." Its lineage descends from Mallarmé's reasons for revising his commemorative sonnet for Verlaine ("Wait . . . let me add at least a little obscurity"), to Eliot's maxim that "genuine poetry can communicate before it is understood," to Stevens' near-quotation of Thoreau: "The poem must resist the intelligence/Almost successfully." For Thoreau, however, the model was not music but the world itself: "We require that all things be mysterious and unexplorable," he writes in "Spring." "We need to witness our own limits transgressed" (213).

Would *Walden*, therefore, have to become as inexplicable as nature? As "obscure"? In fact, however, as so many of its readers have observed, the initial difficulty posed by *Walden* is not obscurity but tedium. Emerson confided to his journal that Thoreau's writing made him "nervous and wretched," and Stanley Cavell, citing that remark, concurs: "It cannot, I think, be denied that *Walden* sometimes seems an enormously long and boring book." We have to confront this problem, and we should ask whether, in Thoreau's case, obscurity and boredom are not distinct issues but *related* ones.

We might start with this observation: almost every reader of *Walden* will discover, on looking back over her copy of the book, that the enthusiastic underlinings and marginal annotations inevitably prompted by the first two chapters trail off in *Walden*'s vast interior, reemerging only with the "Conclusion." The obscurity here seems related to the *purpose* behind the endlessly detailed descriptions that constitute sections like "Sounds," "The Ponds," "Brute Neighbors," and "Winter Animals." "I don't understand," we are tempted to say; "I don't see the point." Writing about Thoreau's *Journals*, the source for *Walden*, Sharon Cameron notes "the progressive refusal to interpret the observations recorded, as if the significance of the description of a tree were the description of that tree."

Cavell and others have alerted us to Thoreau's propensity for the puns and homonyms that revive a word's earlier meaning: in *Walden*, "premises," "present," and "track," among so many others, shift back and forth, conveying now one thing and then another. Thus, we might expect that when Thoreau worries that he has not achieved *obscurity*, he would have in mind not only that word's secondary sense ("not clearly understandable") but also its primary ones: *darkness, remoteness* (in Webster's definition, being "withdrawn from the centers of human activity"). Was *Walden* inadequately "obscure" because the pond was too close to Concord? Were the woods insufficiently dark?

This double sense of *obscurity* hovers around "The Village" passage describing a late-night return to the cabin:

> It was very pleasant, when I staid late in town, to launch myself into the night, especially if it was dark and tempestuous, and set sail from some bright village parlor or lecture room . . . for my snug harbor in the woods. . . . It is darker in the woods, even in common nights, than most suppose. I frequently had to look up

at the opening between the trees above the path in order to learn my route, and, where there was no cart-path, to feel with my feet the faint track which I had worn, or steer by the known relation of particular trees which I felt with my hands, passing between two pines for instance, not more than eighteen inches apart, in the midst of the woods, invariably, in the darkest night. (116–17)

In "Where I Lived and What I Lived For," Thoreau again describes the woods-village opposition in terms of darkness and light: "I was really there," he writes, "or at an equal remoteness from the life which I had left behind, dwindled and twinkling" (63).

Walden's success depends on its becoming less a simple description of Thoreau's experience in the woods than a *simulation* of that experience, one that requires the reader to replicate Thoreau's twenty-six month residence in an intermittently unfamiliar territory. The book's first two chapters, the ones we underline, were written for the public Lyceum lectures he hoped his Concord neighbors would attend. They rely on familiar genres: the sermon, the expository essay, the summons to a better life. *They amount to the town, which will be left behind.* As we abandon them and move away from Concord, we gradually lose the light from the village (the first two chapters) and begin to wander in *Walden's* interior chapters as Thoreau wandered in the woods. We have to learn how to make our way in the book just as Thoreau had to learn how to live away from Concord. It was not easy: "An old-fashioned man," he admits, "would have lost his senses or died of ennui" (90). And the reader's task is equally difficult: as Cavell puts it, "Nothing *holds* my interest, no suspense of plot or development of character." Just as Thoreau's effort involved using detailed observation to retune himself to the natural world, ours requires an adjustment to his frequency, the unfamiliar rhythm and pace, the potential "ennui" of *Walden's* middle sections. For Thoreau, the goal was to love the present moment even when *nothing was happening*: "Sometimes, in a summer morning . . . I sat in my sunny doorway from sunrise till noon, rapt in a revery, amidst the pines and hickories and sumachs, in undisturbed solitude and stillness, while the birds sang around or flitted noiseless through the house" (79). At such moments, the world around him became "like an atmosphere sustaining me" (92). *Walden's* goal is to bring its reader to the experience of that atmosphere so that it will sustain him even when he becomes "a sojourner in civilized life again" (5)—when as Thoreau left the woods, he leaves the book.

(with Lauren Lester)

25.

OPPORTUNITY

Mem. There never is but one opportunity of a kind. (153)

Walden tells the story of a triumph: "I learned this, at least, by my experiment," Thoreau declares in his "Conclusion," "that if one advances confidently in the direction of his dreams, and endeavors to live the life which he has imagined, he will meet with a success unexpected in common hours" (217). For Thoreau, this success was the discovery that he would henceforth be able to avoid regular work; even more important, he had fashioned a way of living and writing that, by tuning his disposition to the natural world, would provide him with satisfaction and even joy. He had reason to brag like chanticleer about what he had found in the woods.

And yet there had always been other possible versions of this story. The deaths of his brother and sister, the *Week*'s absolute commercial failure, the seven-year struggle to complete *Walden,* his neighbors' persistent doubts, his own intermittent melancholy—all these things Thoreau suppressed. "If the reader think that I am vainglorious, and set myself above others," he confided in a passage cut from *Walden,* "I assure him that I could tell a pitiful story respecting myself, . . . could encourage him with a sufficient list of failures. . . . Finally, I will tell him this secret, if he will not abuse my confidence—I put the best face on the matter." This passage, one of the most revealing Thoreau ever wrote, confirms that despite its opening warranty of truthfulness, *Walden* was constructed like a fiction.

Walden is shadowed by other American stories of men who break with all they know and find themselves adrift. Washington Irving's Rip Van Winkle, a town disgrace beloved by children and with "an insuperable aversion to all kinds of profitable labour," chooses to "stroll away into the woods" to avoid farmwork and his wife's nagging. Spellbound by a magic potion, he sleeps away twenty years, awakening to discover that he has lost his youth and his identity: like *It's a Wonderful Life's* George Bailey, he is reduced to pleading: "Does nobody know poor Rip Van Winkle!" Hawthorne's Wakefield leaves home on a business trip, only to take up residence for twenty years (that number again) in an adjacent block, from which he can observe his house and grieving wife. Having had no real reason for this mysterious flight, he needs none to return, but his wife has ceased loving him, and he has become an old man. Melville's Bartleby, a New York clerk, makes an internal retreat by simply refusing everything with the phrase "I would prefer not to." He starves himself to death.

These are cautionary tales. As Hawthorne advises, "Amid the seeming confusion of our mysterious world, individuals are so nicely adjusted to a system, and systems to one another and to a whole, that, by stepping aside for a moment, a man exposes himself to a fearful risk of losing his place forever." Thoreau, however, was not "nicely adjusted" to the system of Concord, and he seemed willing to accept the risk of becoming an outcast. "I do not propose to write an ode to dejection" (60), he announces, having taken pains to avoid the pitfalls. As if alluding to Rip Van Winkle's perilous twenty-year sleep, *Walden* celebrates alertness, insisting that "we must learn to reawaken and keep ourselves awake" (64). Thoreau replaces the capriciousness of Wakefield's adventure with his own sustained purposefulness. And if Bartleby can only say "no," *Walden* records Thoreau's efforts to live according to his own precept, announced in his first published essay: "Surely joy is the condition of life." Thus, among these narratives, *Walden* stands out as the success story, the one that turns out well. Its ability to do so depends on Thoreau's single most decisive move: his conversion of what had begun as pure escape ("Finding that my fellow citizens were not likely to offer me any room in the court house, or any curacy or living any where else, . . . I turned my face more exclusively than ever to the woods" [16]) into a deliberate experiment, designed both to prove his economic hypothesis and to help him discover a way of life. It's as if Wakefield had miraculously found happiness in the house around the corner.

After *Walden*'s first two chapters have confirmed Thoreau's ideas about money and work, the book's experiment turns on revising the sense of the word *opportunity*. When Channing's visit interrupts an irretrievable mood, Thoreau despairs:

> Let me see; where was I? Methinks I was nearly in this frame of mind: the world lay at this angle. Shall I go to heaven or a-fishing? If I should soon bring this meditation to an end, would another so sweet occasion be likely to offer? I was as near being resolved into the essence of things as ever I was in my life. I fear my thoughts will not come back to me. If it would do any good, I would whistle for them. When they make us an offer, is it wise to say, We will think of it? My thoughts have left no track, and I cannot find my path again. . . . Mem. There never is but one opportunity of a kind. (152–53)

This is merely a negative lesson, an example of opportunity's evanescence. To benefit from it, Thoreau had to recognize that the present moment affords fresh opportunities at every instant. "The present was my next experiment of this kind" (60), he declares, after settling economic matters. By his penultimate chapter, he is ready to announce the new moral: "We should be blessed if we lived in the present always, and took advantage of every accident that befell us . . . and did not spend our time atoning for the neglect of past opportunities, which we call doing our duty" (211).

Even Thoreau found this advice more easily said than done. By eliminating distractions, the Walden experiment created a controlled world in which opportunities would regularly appear. But as he confided to his journal, he still had to learn how to attend to them:

> The art of spending a day. If it is possible that we may be addressed, it behooves us to be attentive. If by watching all day and all night I may detect some trace of the Ineffable, then will it not be worth my while to watch? . . .
>
> If by patience, if by watching, I can secure one new ray of light,

can feel myself elevated for an instant upon Pisgah, the world which was dead prose to me becomes living and divine, shall I not watch ever? shall I not be a watchman henceforth? If by watching a whole year on the city's walls I may obtain a communication from heaven, shall I not do well to shut up my shop and turn a watchman? . . .

My profession is to be always on the alert to find God in nature, to know his lurking-places, to attend all the oratories. (*J*, 7 September 1851)

It's a demanding profession, and Thoreau had to train himself to practice it. *Walden* is the record of that training, a manual of drills for alertness, purpose, and affirmation. It is also the antidote to Irving, Hawthorne, and Melville. Thoreau seems even to have intuitively recognized the value of dividing Rip Van Winkle's and Wakefield's sojourns by ten. He was ready to leave the woods after two years: "Perhaps if I lived there much longer I might live there forever. One would think twice before he accepted heaven on such terms" (*J*, 22 January 1852).

(with Kimberly Hunter, Paul Johnson, and Lizzie Paulus)

P

26.

PHILOSOPHER

Compare the following:

Thoreau: To be a philosopher is not merely to have subtle thoughts, nor even to found a school, but so to love wisdom as to live according to its dictates, a life of simplicity, independence, magnanimity, and trust. It is to solve some of the problems of life, not only theoretically, but practically (13).

Nietzsche: I have at all times written my works with my whole body and my whole life; I don't know any "purely intellectual problems."

Wittgenstein: My father was a business man, and I am a business man: I want my philosophy to be businesslike, to get something done, to get something settled.

Following his fellow Viennese Sigmund Freud, Wittgenstein conceived of philosophy as a kind of *therapy*, one that would bring relief from certain torments brought on by language's misuse. (Because language enables us to say that a "mathematical problem" has a solution, we assume that other nouns, like "life," do as well.) What would this "therapy" have done for Thoreau? Prevented his going to Walden? Forestalled his Platonic urge to read Nature symbolically? Diagnosed his post-Walden depression as resulting from the idea of a single, elusive "solution" to life? Or would Wittgenstein have seen Thoreau as a precursor, similarly devoted to solitude, austerity, walking, and handiwork? For this Thoreau, Walden was less theory than practice: there, he became a writer, a citizen, and a business-man, thereby solving simultaneously the practical problems of voca-tion, reputation, and income. He had, in effect, redefined the crucial term: "The economy of living," he now maintained, "is synonymous with philosophy" (39).

Wittgenstein expressed the same attitude. "What is the use of studying philosophy," he once angrily asked his friend Norman Malcolm, "if all that it does for you is to enable you to talk with some plausibility about some abstruse questions of logic, etc., & if it does not improve your thinking about the important questions of everyday life?" Wittgenstein, however, cautioned against mistaking a homemade method for the discovery of "the meaning of life":

> Suppose someone thinks he has found the solution to the "prob-lem of life" and tells himself that now everything is quite easy. To see his error he only has to remind himself that there was a time when this "solution" had not been discovered; but even at *that* time people also had to live. In that light the solution he has dis-covered seems something quite inessential.

Did Thoreau think that with *Walden*, he had solved all of life's ques-tions? He has occasional bouts of modesty: "There are as many ways as there can be drawn radii from one centre" (11), he admits, insist-ing further that "I would not have any one adopt *my* mode of living on any account" (52). But the *I* that begins *Walden* ("In most books, the *I*, or first person, is omitted; in this it will be retained" [5]) often gives way to *you*, the second person that opens up the imperative, the direct address to "you who read these pages" (6), which occa-sionally become a sermon.

Walden's sermon, however, preaches not a doctrine but a *prac-tice*. As Wittgenstein would do in the next century, Thoreau was reconceiving the role of the philosopher, who would now become, in Wittgenstein's words, someone who "demonstrate[s] a method, by examples, and the series of examples can be broken off." This way of working can be puzzling. Confronted by Wittgenstein's meticulous analysis of particular language games (e.g., a tribe of builders using only a handful of words, an order for five red apples), his students could feel lost:

> It was hard to see where all this often rather repetitive concrete detailed talk was leading to—how the examples were interconnected and how all this bore on the problem which one was accustomed to put to oneself in abstract terms.

As Wittgenstein himself admitted about his *Philosophical Investigations,* "If this book is written as it should be written, then everything I say must be easily understandable . . . but it should be difficult to understand *why* I say it." This remark gets at one of *Walden's* basic problems. As the book leaves behind its first two chapters, originally designed as Lyceum lectures, to embark on detailed accounts of fishing at night, a locomotive's sounds, the pond's colors in various lights, the dates of first freezes, a loon's skittering across the water, *Walden* becomes less a syllogistic argument than a relentless accumulation: "And then I did this; and then I heard this; and then I saw this." None of these passages is hard to understand, but as they drone on, nearly all *Walden* readers will find themselves asking, "Why does Thoreau *need* to tell me these things?"

It's a new way of doing philosophy, and even Emerson didn't get it. Thoreau was practicing a method Wittgenstein would explain: "In order to see more clearly . . . we must focus on the details of what goes on; must look at them *from close up.*" *Walden's* inner chapters render precisely that kind of *close up* looking, but what that looking revealed can be shown more than said. That showing, however, takes time and in doing so, threatens to exasperate even Thoreau's most sympathetic reader.

Walden represents Thoreau's attempt "to solve some of the problems of life, not only theoretically, but practically" (13). Having worked out a method for doing so, he faced what Cavell calls the problem of establishing "his right to declare it." Wittgenstein's appropriation of the businessman analogy suggests Thoreau's solution. By describing his own "economical" practices, Thoreau deposits the collateral required to secure the loan of our attention: look, he says, I'm not some head-in-the-clouds philosopher—I can build a house, plant a crop, mend my clothes, find my way home through the woods in the dark. "I have always endeavored to acquire strict business habits" (17), he points out to any of his readers who might regard philosophy as insufficiently "practical" and "hard headed" compared to money making. He insists on knowing the real cost of things, always less a matter of money than life. The lesson is stern, and as Richard J. Schneider has observed, although Thoreau's churchgoing neighbors were used to being denounced as sinful, they would have felt shock at being called foolish. But Thoreau offers his philosophy as the most practical of them all. In his second letter to Harrison Blake, he asks the question most important to this new image of the philosopher:

> I know many men who, in common things, are not to be deceived; who trust no moonshine; who count their money correctly, and know how to invest it; who are said to be prudent and know-ing, who yet will stand at a desk the greater part of their lives, as cashiers in banks, and glimmer and rust and finally go out there. If they *know* anything, what under the sun do they do that for?
>
> *(with Adam Nikolaidis)*

27

PROVING

Perhaps because *Walden* is such an obviously ambitious book with a determinedly elevated tone, Thoreau quickly acquired a reputation as a ponderous, humorless writer. After accusing Thoreau of "gutting" his works of anything that might make his readers laugh, Robert Louis Stevenson remarked that "he was not one of those authors who have learned . . . 'to leave out the dullness.'" Writing in 1880, just eighteen years after Thoreau's death, Stevenson was following the example of James Russell Lowell, who in 1865 had flatly declared that "Thoreau had no humor." Emerson never mentioned *Walden,* even in his own journals. Although he accused Thoreau of lacking "a lyric facility and technical skill," he preferred his friend's poetry to his prose, which he thought marred by reflexive paradox. In the twentieth century, Leon Edel summarized the case against Thoreau, curtly declaring, "He was not a born writer."

This last judgment, leveled at the author of at least one classic book and a two-million-word journal, now seems astonishingly off. We should remember, however, that several of Thoreau's contemporaries demonstrated that prolificness does not inevitably signal talent: Margaret Fuller, William Ellery Channing, and Henry James Sr. all wrote at unembarrassed length without showing any natural affinity for literature. Thoreau, on the other hand, may have been one of those writers like Whitman or Neruda (but unlike T. S. Eliot) who need to write a lot in order to produce a small amount of first-rate work: even *Walden*'s greatest admirers have never made similar claims for the *Week, The Maine Woods,* or *Cape Cod.*

What in Thoreau's work were Emerson, Lowell, Stevenson, and Edel responding to? Although it has become a classic, *Walden* rarely seems light and effortless. We know, of course, that it wasn't: Thoreau took seven years and seven drafts to finish it, constructing the book from journal entries and lectures composed over an even longer stretch. This is a recurring pattern with Thoreau: Robert Richardson repeatedly uses the phrase "worked up" to describe Thoreau's method of turning earlier material into publishable form. Even his apparently offhand journal resulted from carefully revised notes, usually taken the day before. Despite his deafness to Thoreau, Lowell diagnosed the problem: "Neither his attention nor his genius was of the spontaneous kind."

Roland Barthes distinguished between "a labor of knowledge" and a labor "of writing," defining the latter, "poetic" mode, which he preferred, as "any discourse in which the word leads the idea." Almost any writer would recognize what Barthes was getting at: writing takes off when you yield the initiative to rhythms and words, but having a point to make can turn it into a torturous translation process, a struggle to find the verbal analogue for something already floating around in your head. When Degas complained to Mallarmé about his inability to write good sonnets, despite "having so many ideas," the poet replied, "You don't make sonnets with ideas, Degas, but with words." Like Degas's poetry, Thoreau's work often seems to have been "a labor of knowledge": he had things to say or experiences to describe. Thus, when he describes waking at night with "a statement which I had never consciously considered before, and as surprising and novel and agreeable to me as anything can be" (as close as Thoreau gets to automatic writing), he explains the phenomenon as the result of previous thought: "There is such a necessity [to] make a definite statement that our minds at length do it without our consciousness" (*J*, 1 April 1860). Even Thoreau's excursions—to Maine, Canada, Cape Cod, and Walden itself—were designed less for themselves than as ways to acquire raw material for writing. An assignment set for a friend indicates Thoreau's own method:

> Let me suggest a theme for you—to state to yourself precisely and
> completely what that walk over the mountains amounted to for
> you, returning to this essay again and again until you are satisfied

that all that was important in your experience is in it. Don't suppose that you can tell it precisely the first dozen times you try, but at 'em again; especially when, after a sufficient pause, you suspect that you are touching the heart or summit of the matter, reiterate your blows there, and account for the mountain to yourself. Not that the story need be long, but it will take a long while to make it short.

Despite Thoreau's love of poetry and languages, he seems to have liked ideas and nature even more. His reading matter, exhaustively detailed by Robert Richardson, was often not only remarkably dull but surprisingly "unliterary": can something like *Reports—on the Fishes, Reptiles, and Birds; the Herbaceous Plants and Quadrupeds; the Insects Injurious to Vegetation; and the Invertebrate Animals—of Massachusetts* be classified as anything but "a labor of knowledge"? In places, however, he appears to have sought a different way of working. "Obey the spur of the moment," he advises himself. "These accumulated it is that makes the impulse and the impetus of the life of genius" (*J*, 26 January 1852). While this maxim applies more to living than to writing, Thoreau occasionally turns it into a compositional strategy:

Write often, write upon a thousand themes, rather than long at a time, not trying to turn to[o] many feeble somersets in the air. . . . Those sentences are good and well discharged which are like so many little resiliencies from the spring floor of our life. . . . Sentences uttered with your back to the wall. (*J*, 12 November 1851)

This last sentence is Thoreau at his best—vivid, martial, surprising. At *its* best, *Walden* works similarly, allowing language to generate an argument rather than simply translate it. Thus Thoreau's "economy" seems prompted by the various, and sometimes contradictory, meanings of certain words: *business, capital, cost, enterprise, interest.* In other places, the book's wit derives from a deliberate ambiguity, as in its fourth sentence, whose final adjective can refer to four different antecedents ("my affairs," the "very particular inquiries," "my townsmen," or "my mode of life"):

> I should not obtrude my affairs so much on the notice of my read-
> ers if very particular inquiries had not been made by my towns-
> men concerning my mode of life, which some would call imperti-
> nent. (5)

Similarly, when Thoreau writes that he "walked over each farmer's *premises*" (58, emphasis added), he wants us to recognize that prop-erty is not only land, but also the presupposition of a life.

Thoreau is always ready to exploit a pun. Observing the pickerel swimming under the pond's frozen surface, he notes that "They, of course, are Walden all over and all through" (191), playing on the lake's name as a homonym of *walled in*. "I have thoroughly tried school-keeping" (50), he writes, evoking his own last name, which his family pronounced as *thorough*. Thus, we should be alert to the other meanings available in one of his favorite words: *improve*.

> I do not speak to those who are well employed . . . but mainly to
> the mass of men who are discontented, and idly complaining of
> the hardness of their lot or of the times, when they might improve
> them. (14)

The *Walden* experiment was, from the start, an effort to improve his own lot: "In any weather, at any hour of the day or night," Thoreau declares, "I have been anxious to improve the nick of time, and notch it on my stick too" (14). Or, more obscurely: "That time which we really improve, or which is improvable, is neither past, present, nor future" (71).

Thoreau suggests that by building and planting on Emerson's land, he was *improving* it. But he also needed to improve himself. The year before, he and Edward Hoar had accidently set fire to over three hundred acres of neighboring woods, an act described by the Concord newspaper as "sheer carelessness," resulting from "the thoughtlessness of two of our citizens." He had begun to exhaust Emerson's patience, and his own literary and teaching careers had reached dead ends. He would turn twenty-eight a week after taking up his residence at the pond, but the venture smacked of adoles-cent bravado. As Leon Edel observes, it resembled the act of a "child saying, in effect, to the town and to Emerson, 'see how homeless I am, you have forced me to live in a shanty away from all of you.'" Thoreau knew, however, that if he could make his experiment pay off, he would justify himself. Thus, when he writes *improving*, we should also hear *I'm proving*—my genius, my economy, my skills, my character, myself.

(with Craig Cieslikowski)

28.

QUESTION

After a still winter night I awoke with the impression that some question had been put to me, which I had been endeavoring in vain to answer in my sleep, as what—how—when—where? But there was dawning Nature, in whom all creatures live, looking in at my broad windows with serene and satisfied face, and no question on her lips. I awoke to an answered question, to Nature and daylight. The snow lying deep on the earth dotted with young pines, and the very slope of the hill on which my house is placed, seem to say, Forward! Nature puts no question and answers none which we mortals ask. (189)

This lovely, mysterious passage, both as hushed and as brazen as a cold-bright winter day, suggests an alternative to the standard image of Thoreau the spiritual explorer who, after the Elysian Fields of Walden Pond, would watch his own imaginative powers steadily diminish. Sherman Paul, who most eloquently diagnoses this melancholy position, observes that "after *Walden* . . . his *Journals* became increasingly a repository of scientific facts. . . . Where once he had told how the summer felt to him, he now merely recorded the temperature." For Paul, "the considerable barrenness of these *Journals*" attests to Thoreau's inability to recapture the "extended ecstasy" of the woods, those "rare intervals" he had described in *A Week on the Concord and Merrimack Rivers,* when "we rise above the necessity of virtue into an unchangeable morning light, in which we have only to live right on and breathe the ambrosial air" (*Week,* 369).

Thoreau's own words occasionally confirm this picture, especially the wistful 19 August 1851 journal entry so often cited by its proponents: "I fear that the character of my knowledge is from year to year becoming more distinct and scientific; that, in exchange for views as wide as heaven's cope, I am being narrowed down to the field of the microscope. I see details, not whole nor the shadow of the whole." But "The Pond in Winter" provides a different clue about what it would mean "to live right on and breathe the ambrosial air." From this perspective, Thoreau appears as a man deflected from his own instinctive love of nature and natural history by a Harvard education and Emerson's influence. Significantly, his first major essay, "Natural History of Massachusetts," seems content to devote itself almost entirely to botanical and zoological description. Only in the last paragraph does the famous sentence appear: "Let us not underrate the value of a fact; it will one day flower in a truth." What, however, was that truth to be? In one sense, Thoreau designed the Walden experiment to answer that question. "I went to the woods because I wished to live deliberately, to front only the essential facts of life, and see if I could not learn what it had to teach" (65), he writes in *Walden*'s second chapter. "The Pond in Winter" passage, however, suggests that the answer lay in abandoning the question and with it, Emerson's kind of philosophizing. He announced this new program in the *Week:* "The wisest man preaches no doctrines; he has no schemes; he sees no rafter, not even a cobweb, against the heavens. It is clear sky" (70).

In bringing this other picture of Thoreau into focus, no writer is more helpful that Wittgenstein. As Katherine Morris and Gordon Baker have pointed out, Wittgenstein, following Freud's example, describes philosophy's proper role as *therapy,* designed only for those tormented by philosophical problems that cause "particular personal disquiets." "The way I do philosophy," Wittgenstein writes, "its whole job is to frame an expression in such a way that certain worries disappear." As Baker explains,

> Such questions are regarded as tokens of the questioner's intellectual disquiet, sometimes even terror or anxiety. They arise from *intellectual* obsessions, compulsions or "neuroses." . . . Such questions need to be *dis*solved rather than solved or answered.

Baker is using Wittgenstein's own simile: "The problems," Wittgenstein insists, "are, in the strict sense, dissolved like a piece of sugar in water." And this process is achieved "not by giving new information, but by arranging what we have always known." The method will require the description of meticulously observed examples.

The parallel with Thoreau is striking. Just as Wittgenstein's thinking arose from his own philosophical torment, Thoreau's anxious need for both a vocation and wisdom prompted the Walden experiment. In effect, both were desperate men. Like Wittgenstein, Thoreau quickly acknowledges that not everyone will need his therapy: "I do not mean to prescribe rules to strong and valiant natures, who will mind their own affairs" (14), he writes in his book's first chapter; the real audience is "the mass of men who are discontented," presumably including himself. His method, anticipating Wittgenstein's, lies in deploying a detailed description of his twenty-six months at the pond to effect what Wittgenstein calls an "aspect change," the revelation that our own worlds, our own neighborhoods, the most ordinary events of everyday life are "a miracle which is taking place every instant" (11). Wittgenstein would later insist that "the aspects of things that are most important for us are hidden because of their simplicity and familiarity. (One is unable to notice something— because it is always before one's eyes)." *Walden* makes that lesson rhapsodic:

> In eternity there is indeed something true and sublime. But all
> these times and places and occasions are now and here, God him-
> self culminates in the present moment, and will never be more
> divine in the lapse of all the ages. (69)

Wittgenstein objected to traditional philosophy's reliance on arcane terminology; "the old familiar words of the language are quite sufficient." For his part, Thoreau replaced the exotic and extraordinary with the homely and familiar: "I omit the unusual," he confided to his journal while writing *Walden*: "The hurricanes and earthquakes and describe the common. This . . . is the true theme of poetry" (J, 28 August 1851). Indeed, Thoreau's salvation begins when he anticipates Wittgenstein's advice about a certain kind of anxiety:

The peculiarity of philosophical worry and its resolution might seem to be that it is like the anguish of an ascetic, groaning under the weight of a heavy sphere, until someone gives him relief by saying "let it drop."

For Thoreau, "letting it drop" involved relinquishing the project of making every fact flower into a truth: "I begin to see . . . objects only when I leave off understanding them" (*J*, 14 February 1851).

At their most severe, both Thoreau and Wittgenstein could write dismissively of those who did not feel the urgency of the questions that worried them. "I do not say that John or Jonathan will realize all this" (224), Thoreau concludes, implying, of course, that they *should*. Wittgenstein is more harsh:

Some philosophers (or whatever you like to call them) suffer from what may be called "loss of problems." Then everything seems quite simple to them, no deep problems seem to exist any more, the world becomes broad and flat and loses all depth, and what they write becomes immeasurably shallow and trivial.

"Shallow and trivial" is exactly how most commentators have described Thoreau's post-1854 *Journal*. But if "The Pond in Winter" passage that heads this entry in any indication, a "loss of problems" does not necessarily entail a defeat. Instead, it marks Thoreau's successful retuning to the world's frequency, his acceptance of Nature on its own terms, without any particular meaning. "The best thought is not only without somberness," he had written in 1841, "but without morality. The universe lies outspread in floods of white light to it. The moral aspect of nature is a disease caught of man" (*J*, 1 August 1841). Thoreau would not retreat from this position. He wrote to B. B. Wiley in 1856 that "I do not now remember anything which Confucius has said directly regarding man's 'origin, purpose, and destiny.' He was more practical than that." The same letter proposes that Swedenborg's addressing these problems "is not *altogether* a recommendation; since such an answer to these questions cannot be discovered, any more than perpetual motion, for which no reward is now offered." "Walking," one of Thoreau's last essays, makes his rejection of "philosophical questions" explicit:

My desire for knowledge is intermittent, but my desire to bathe my head in atmospheres unknown to my feet is perennial and constant. The highest that we can attain to is not Knowledge, but Sympathy with Intelligence. I do not know that this higher knowledge amounts to anything more definite than a novel and grand surprise on a sudden revelation of the insufficiency of all that we called Knowledge before,—a discovery that there are more things in heaven and earth than are dreamed of in our philosophy. It is the lighting up of the mist by the sun.

Wittgenstein, of course, seemed to reach the same point: one of his most famous remarks repeats Thoreau's ecstatic celebration of the questions' vanishing and treats the "loss of problems" as the answer after all:

For the clarity we are aiming at is indeed *complete* clarity. But this simply means that the philosophical problems should *completely* disappear.

The real discovery is the one that makes me capable of stopping doing philosophy when I want to.—The one that gives philosophy peace, so that it is no longer tormented by questions.

One day at Walden, Thoreau awoke to the world around him, and for the moment at least, the philosophical questions he had inherited from Emerson vanished in the cold, clear morning air.

R

29.

READERS

Because *Walden*'s growing popularity has often derived from Thoreau's advocacy of certain issues, especially civil disobedience and environmentalism, we have tended to avoid a central problem: what is Thoreau's relationship to his readers? It's not an easy question to answer. *Walden* is at once inspirational and demoralizing, revelatory and boring, practical and quixotic; and Thoreau himself appears as a prophet, companion, scold, laborer, idler, eccentric, businessman, braggart, nature lover, and instructor. What reader is sufficiently *thorough* (to evoke his name's Concord pronunciation) to accommodate all these attitudes and roles? *Walden,* in other words, not only represents Thoreau's solution to his own problem of writing; it also poses a problem of reading: who can read *Walden* correctly?

Walden is an instruction manual, but it is also a sermon, offering the standard fire-and-brimstone rebuke before its summons to the True Way. "There is not one of my readers," Thoreau announces, "who has yet lived a whole human life" (223), a relatively mild invective compared to others, where general propositions snap suddenly into direct address:

> The mass of men lead lives of quiet desperation. What is called resignation is confirmed desperation. From the desperate city you go into the desperate country, and have to console yourself with the bravery of minks and muskrats. (8–9)

In other places, Thoreau skips the indirection: "It is very evident what mean and sneaking lives many of you live," he admonishes. And he does not spare himself: "Why do you stay here and live this mean moiling life," he asks of his pseudonym "John Farmer," "when a glorious existence is possible for you?" (151). At times, he despairs of all humanity: "To be awake is to be alive. I have never yet met a man who was quite awake. How could I have looked him in the face?" (64). In the face of this condition, Thoreau offers a preacher's typically strenuous moral: "Nature is hard to overcome, but she must be overcome" (150).

Like all good sermons, however, *Walden* offers a regimen of salvation and a promise of glory: "I learned this, at least by my experiment," Thoreau concludes; "that if one advances confidently in the direction of his dreams, and endeavors to live the life which he has imagined, he will meet with a success unexpected in common hours" (217). While Thoreau's churchgoing contemporaries would almost certainly have recognized *Walden*'s appropriations of the sermon's tone, they would have been discomforted by the book's secular conclusion that "heaven is under our feet as well as over our heads" (190), that "Olympus is but the outside of the earth every where" (61). Now, in this post-Nietzschean world, it is Thoreau's regimen that troubles us: "Our lives must be stripped" (29). Thoreau went about the stripping: he had no wife, no children, no regular job; from his diet, he eliminated meat, fish, salt, sugar, yeast, coffee, tea, and wine. (Some speculation suggests that malnourishment may have contributed to his tuberculosis.) He kept his clothes and shoes until they wore out. In *Walden,* he proposes that a man could live comfortably in one of the six-by-three-feet boxes where railroad workers stored their tools, and after insisting that "this did not appear the worst, nor by any means a despicable alternative," he assures his readers that "I am far from jesting" (23).

Thoreau's impossible austerity has its precedent in Jesus's uncompromising warning: "If any man come to me, and hate not his father, and mother, and wife, and children, and brethren, and sisters, yea, and his own life also, he cannot be my disciple" (Luke 14: 26). In "Walking," a posthumously published essay that began as an 1851 lecture, Thoreau would echo those words:

If you are ready to leave father and mother, and brother and sister, and wife and child and friends, and never see them again,—if you have paid your debts, and made your will, and settled all your affairs, and are a free man, then you are ready for a walk.

It's an impossible requirement, and the practical New England businessmen who heard it preached on Sunday knew how to forget it during the week. Christianity's general tenets may have remained alive, but the details of its practice did not. As with Jesus's teaching, *Walden*'s counsel survives in its outlines: wakefulness, simplicity, purposefulness. But to the extent that *Walden* has become, for many readers, a sacred text, another Bible, it has also turned into something Thoreau never wanted it to be: an *impractical* book.

(with Paul Johnson)

30

RENTS

This car-load of torn sails is more legible and interesting now than if they should be wrought into paper and printed books. Who can write so graphically the history of the storms they have weathered as these rents have done? They are proof-sheets which need no correction. (84)

This passage appears in "Sounds," a chapter that begins by unfavorably comparing "written languages" to "the language which all things and events speak without metaphor" (78). For this seemingly unimaginable possibility, Thoreau offers the example of torn sails, whose rents provide the direct indexical traces of hard weather, the world's account of itself rather than one provided by a human mediator. In admiring this elimination of human expression, Thoreau was anticipating the capacities André Bazin attributed to the camera. "For the first time," Bazin wrote in 1945, "an image of the world is formed automatically, without the creative intervention of man." Bazin's analogies for the photograph all emphasized the unmediated imprinting of the world on the camera's chemically treated paper: the resulting image is "a kind of decal or transfer," the veil of Veronica, the holy shroud of Turin, an embalmed version of what had occurred before its lens. Bazin celebrated filmmakers who recognized what the camera can do and knew enough to stay out of the way. "Rossellini directs facts," Bazin wrote, offering his highest praise.

In places, Thoreau sounds as if he wanted to be a camera. Longing for "a fact truly and adequately stated," he proposed a Bazinian method: "Say it and have done with it. Express it without expressing yourself" (*J*, 1 November 1851). Thoreau, however, had also been too influenced by romanticism to renounce Wordsworth's lesson that "the mind is lord and master—outward sense/The obedient servant of her will" (*The Prelude*, 12. 222–23). At the least, *Walden* enacts Wordsworth's counsel to

> maintain
> A balance, an ennobling interchange
> Of action from without and from within;
> The excellence, pure function, and best power
> Both of the object seen, and eye that sees.
>
> (*The Prelude*, 13. 374–78)

In fact, writing became for Thoreau more than a way of transcribing an experience; it was also his means of having an experience in the first place. "How many communications may we not lose through inattention?" he asked himself. "I would fain keep a journal which should contain those thoughts and impressions which I am most liable to forget that I have had; which would have in one sense the greatest remoteness, in another, the greatest nearness to me" (*J*, 10 January 1851). Thus, although *Walden* as a book rarely makes any mention of Thoreau's writing, the Walden experiment depended on it.

(with Charles Meyer)

31

RUINS

In "Former Inhabitants and Winter Visitors," Thoreau observes, "I am not aware that any man has ever built on the spot which I occupy," a statement that provokes a creed:

Deliver me from a city built on the site of a more ancient city, whose materials are ruins, whose gardens cemeteries. The soil is blanched and accursed there. (178)

Walden, however, a book so full of allusions that it requires extensive footnotes, is itself an edifice "constructed on the site of a more ancient city," the "heroic books" (71) Thoreau so often celebrates. In his repudiation of the Old World's cities and his desire for a fresh start, Thoreau is typically American. But his reverence for older writers and their sacred texts, his devotion to learning, resemble a classicist's deference. By using the boards from James Collins's shanty for his own cabin, Thoreau had shown that he could build something new—something better, cleaner, more "economical"—out of something old. In building *Walden,* he intended to do the same thing.

Emerson recalled having once asked Thoreau, "Who would not like to write something we can all read, like *Robinson Crusoe*?" Thoreau appears to have seized on this offhand remark. Although he boasted that he had "never read a novel," he almost certainly had read *Robinson Crusoe,* mentioned not only in his *Journal* (J, 22 February 1841), but also in the *Week* (290) and "Ktaadn." *Walden* contains the obvious *Crusoe* reference ("I have been anxious to improve the nick of time, and notch it on my stick too" [14]), but more importantly, it minimizes accounts of Thoreau's near-daily visits to town, thereby painting a picture of "heroic" solitude. Thoreau, in other words, used Defoe's novel as the foundation for his own structure.

In Cato the Elder's classic treatise on farming, *De re rustica,* Thoreau found an even more immediate foundation for *Walden.* Thoreau acknowledged Cato's text as "my 'Cultivator'" (60), and he thoroughly relied on it. Thoreau's opening salvo, "Economy," with its attack on business and the accepted professions, follows Cato's preface dismissing trade as an insecure occupation prone to disaster. Yet both authors apply a scrupulously businesslike approach to their own accounts: Thoreau's itemized expenditures seem modeled on Cato's detailed list of supplies and expenses. As Thoreau would do in *Walden,* Cato structured *De re rustica* around the seasons, ending with spring. This organizing principle became the frame for Cato's practical philosophical advice, which often sounds Thoreauvian: "In rain, look for work to be done indoors. Rather than do nothing, do cleaning. Remember that the establishment will cost just as much if nothing is done." Cato's culminating advice about the benefits of cabbage seems to have stuck in Thoreau's head: to appreciate the "health-giving properties of cabbage," Cato advised, "you must first know the different kinds of cabbage and their nature," for cabbage is "at once dry and wet." When Emerson used part of his eulogy to criticize Thoreau's paradoxes as "a trick," he offered an example: "It was so dry," he recalled him saying, "that you might call it wet.

(with Brenda Maxey-Billings and Daniel O'Malley)

32.

SPIDER

Do not trouble yourself much to get new things, whether clothes or friends. Turn the old; return to them. Things do not change; we change. Sell your clothes and keep your thoughts. God will see that you do not want society. If I were confined to a corner of a garret all my days, like a *spider*, the world would be just as large to me while I had my thoughts about me. (220)

Walden's "Conclusion" returns to the tone of exhortation with which Thoreau had begun his book seventeen chapters earlier. But while the opening salvos of "Economy" and "Where I Lived and What I Lived For" ring with the morning bravado of the cockcrow ("I do not propose to write an ode to dejection, but to brag as lustily as chanticleer" [60]), *Walden's* final chapter offers a quieter benediction and a different creature for self-comparison. The spider, associated in popular idiom with patience and care, had implicitly appeared in Thoreau's second chapter, where his words "wherever I sat, there I might live, and the landscape radiated from me accordingly" (58) offered the image of a spider spinning its web from a center constituted only by itself. Like a spider, which sets up shop on others' space, Thoreau had cleared, planted, and built on Emerson's land, but the world he had made he called his own.

Where does this spider lead? First, to *The Gay Science*, where Nietzsche proposed "eternal recurrence" as the criterion for judging how one chooses to live:

The greatest weight. What, if some day or night a demon were to steal after you into your loneliest loneliness and say to you: "This life as you now live it and have lived it, you will have to live once more and innumerable times more; and there will be nothing new in it, but every pain and every joy and every thought and sigh and everything unutterably small or great in your life will have to return to you, all in the same succession and sequence—even this *spider* and this moonlight between the trees, and even this moment and I myself. . . ." The question in each and every thing, "Do you desire this once more and innumerable times more?" would lie upon your actions as the greatest weight. Or how well disposed would you have to become to yourself and to life *to crave nothing more fervently* than this ultimate eternal confirmation and seal?

As early as 1842, Thoreau had formulated his own version of this standard, if only to himself: "I wish to communicate those parts of my life which I would gladly live again myself" (*J,* 26 March 1842). In *Walden,* that test has become a strenuous imperative: "Every man is tasked to make his life, even in its details, worthy of the contemplation of his most elevated and critical hour" (65). Two years after *Walden's* publication, however, Thoreau would greet this challenge with sheer exuberance: "I am grateful for what I am and have," he wrote to Harrison Blake. "My thanksgiving is perpetual. . . . I am ready to try this for the next 1000 years, & exhaust it. How sweet to think of!"

In the light thrown back on it by *The Gay Science, Walden* now appears as an anticipation of this doctrine, a book Thoreau began as a Platonist and ended as a Nietzschean. Like Nietzsche, Thoreau rejected the opposition of "real" and "apparent" worlds ("Talk of heaven! ye disgrace earth" [134]), replacing that dialectic, so basic to Western philosophy, with a celebration of this life:

> In eternity there is indeed something true and sublime. But all these times and places and occasions are now and here. God himself culminates in the present moment. (69)

Walden's spider leads to *Charlotte's Web,* whose eponymous hero confirms Thoreau's faith that writing can literally save a life (Charlotte rescues the pig Wilbur simply by writing SOME PIG and TERRIFIC in her web, thereby convincing Wilbur's owner that he has "special properties" that must be preserved and that he must not just be used for bacon). As the dying Charlotte, exhausted by her labors, says farewell to Wilbur, she uses exactly *Walden*'s language of faith in the world and the seasons' perpetual renewal:

Nothing can harm you now. These autumn days will shorten and grow cold. The leaves will shake loose from the trees and fall. Christmas will come, then the snows of winter. You will live to enjoy the beauty of the frozen world, for you mean a great deal to Zuckerman and he will not harm you, ever. Winter will pass, the days will lengthen, the ice will melt in the pasture pond. The song sparrow will return and sing, the frogs will awake, the warm wind will blow again. All these sights and sounds and smells will be yours to enjoy, Wilbur—this lovely world, these precious days.

Two years after the appearance of *Charlotte's Web,* its author, E. B. White, would publish his famous essay honoring *Walden*'s centenary ("Walden—1954"), citing Thoreau's own—tacit—version of the spider ("Wherever I sat, there I might live, and the landscape radiated from me accordingly") and remarking, as if it were a spiderweb, on the simultaneously tough and fragile nature of *Walden* itself: "If it were a little less good than it is, or even a little less queer, it would be an abominable book."

White, of course, was associated primarily with the *New Yorker,* precisely the kind of well-paying, intellectually sophisticated magazine that Thoreau tried desperately to break into during his lost year in New York in 1843. This commercial failure prompted Thoreau's move to Walden Pond eighteen months later. Founded at the height of the jazz age (21 February 1925), the *New Yorker* cultivated an image of wit, worldliness, and urbanity, qualities scorned by Thoreau. Oddly, however, the magazine became the principal site of Thoreau's legacy, the environmental movement. Having published Rachel Carson's *The Sea Around Us* in 1951, *New Yorker* editor William Shawn commissioned her 1962 ecological manifesto "Silent Spring," a fifty-thousand-word essay that first revealed DDT's perils. In 1982, Shawn ran an even longer essay, Jonathan Shell's "The Fate of the Earth," which imagined the fatal consequences of nuclear war. Six years later came "The End of Nature," written by the most radical of the *New Yorker*'s environmentalists, Bill McKibben, whose Thoreauvian views and tone may have cost him the magazine's editorship. In 1997, McKibben wrote an introduction to a new edition of *Walden* in which he argued that "it is most crucial to read *Walden* as a practical environmentalist's volume" asking "two intensely practical questions": "How much is enough? and How do I know what I want?" "If you could answer them," Thoreau had insisted, "you might improve your own life." Now, the planet's fate depends on those answers.

33

STRIPPED

Before we can adorn our houses with beautiful objects the walls
must be stripped, and our lives must be stripped. (29)

Walden's more didactic sections, especially its first two chapters,
repeatedly erase the distinction between practical issues and philosophy. This move, of course, lies at the heart of Thoreau's project,
announced early in "Economy": "To be a philosopher is not merely
to have subtle thoughts, nor even to found a school. . . . It is to solve
some of the problems of life, not only theoretically, but practically"
(13). With Thoreau, there is no necessary priority: either the practical
or the philosophical issue can come first. Thus, the task of building a
house with boards from James Collins's shanty prompts an introductory disquisition on architecture, which, in turn, abruptly becomes a
moral precept: "Our lives must be stripped."

Emerson dismissively suggested that Thoreau found it easy to
follow his own maxim: "He had no temptations to fight against, no
appetites, no passions, no taste for elegant trifles," Emerson wrote in
his eulogy. "He was bred to no profession; he never married; he lived
alone; he never went to church; he never voted; he refused to pay a
tax to the state; he ate no flesh, he drank no wine, he never knew the
use of tobacco." Even to his most sympathetic readers, Thoreau's life
has always seemed remarkably "stripped." Less apparent, however, is
the extent to which Thoreau also "stripped" *Walden*. After promis-
ing "a simple and sincere account" of his own life at the pond, Thoreau offers a book whose lack of intimacy continues to unsettle us.

Thoreau tells few stories, admits to no doubts. He never uses Emerson's name or mentions his own family. Anecdotes about the Collinses' family cat or a hunted fox trail off into dead ends, while others about an "artist of Kouroo" or "a hound, a bay horse, and a turtledove" become opaque parables. Because we have grown so accustomed to *Walden*'s remoteness, we may realize what Thoreau has left out only when we happen upon a *Journal* entry registering his characteristic mood swings:

> For a day or two it has been quite cool, a coolness that was felt even when sitting by an open window in a thin coat on the west side of the house in the morning, and you naturally sought the sun at that hour. The coolness concentrated your thought, however. . . . I feel as if this coolness would do me good. If it only makes my life more pensive! Why should pensiveness be akin to sadness? There is a certain fertile sadness which I would not avoid, but rather earnestly seek. It is positively joyful to me. It saves my life from being trivial. . . . This coolness comes to condense the dews and clear the atmosphere. The stillness seems more deep and significant. Each sound seems to come from out a greater thoughtfulness in nature. . . . My heart leaps into my mouth at the sound of the wind in the woods. I, whose life was but yesterday so desultory and shallow, suddenly recover my spirits, my spirituality. . . . Ah! if I could so live that there should be no desultory moment in all my life! . . . [T]hat I could match nature always with my moods! (*J*, 17 August 1851)

Thoreau's refusal "to write an ode to dejection" (5) insured that such wistful confessions of even fleeting melancholy could find no place in his book. At some point, he seems to have decided that the goal of waking his neighbors up was simply incompatible with any acknowledgment of irresolution. He had to pretend, as Robert Louis Stevenson said of him, that "the needle did not tremble as with richer natures, but pointed steadily north." Thus, *Walden* presents Thoreau's decisions as the inevitable result of a moral imperative, not as a stage in his own interior struggle. The modern novel and memoir have trained us to expect not only action but also the thought behind it. By eliminating almost all of these genre's conventional devices—confession, storytelling, reversals of fortune, indecision, sudden action—Thoreau strips away the trappings of literature as he had the luxuries of life. Thus, with its careful elisions and narrative austerity, *Walden* became an exact analogue of the life Thoreau had cut out for himself in the woods.

(with Brian Brown and Adam Nikolaidis)

T

34.

TRACKS AND PATHS

Thoreau's attention to the Fitchburg train, roaring past five times a day barely six hundred yards from his cabin, moves characteristically from sounds—"the rattle of railroad cars," "the whistle of the locomotive," the earth-shaking thunder of the engine (81–82)—to the word *track* itself, mobilized as a metaphor for deadening routine. Watching the railroad workers ride by prompts the first shift into this other register:

> The men on the freight trains, who go over the whole length of the road, bow to me as an old acquaintance, they pass me so often, and apparently they take me for an employee; and so I am. I too would fain be a track-repairer somewhere in the orbit of the earth. (81)

The train's whistle, a "warning to get off the track" (81), gives Thoreau what he needs, an image of dehumanizing mechanization that "regulates a whole country," an implacable "fate, an *Atropos,* that never turns aside" (83). Stephen Fender has described the railroad's effect on Concord: it enabled the transcendentalists' connection to their Cambridge and Boston colleagues while damaging local businesses suddenly thrown into competition with metropolitan stores. Immediately apparent was the loss of local time, as the railroad's scheduling mandated standardized time zones: with the train's arrival, Thoreau observes, "the farmers set their clocks by them" (83).

Walden always insists that what we call things matters, and "fate" implies that we have no choice about "tracks." In "Economy," however, Thoreau declares that we do. It is one of *Walden*'s most important points:

> But men labor under a mistake. . . . By a seeming fate, commonly called necessity, they are employed, as it says in an old book, laying up treasures which moth and rust will corrupt and thieves break through and steal. It is a fool's life, as they will find when they get to the end of it, if not before. (7)

"The mass of men lead lives of quiet desperation" (8) because they have mistaken their own choices for "fate" or "necessity." If these same men find themselves stuck on a track, perhaps "the beaten track of the professions" (106), all they have to do, Thoreau says, is get off it. "Every path but your own is the path of fate," he writes. "Keep on your own track, then" (83). In effect, *Walden* anticipates Wittgenstein's dictum that "the job to be done in philosophy . . . is really more a job on oneself. On one's viewpoint. On how one sees things. (And what one demands from them.)" Thoreau demands that we see our lives as of our own making.

But in some ways, this reading is too simple. Elsewhere in *Walden*, the word *track* and its synonym *path* appear more favorably. Returning from Concord to his cabin at night, when "it is darker in the woods . . . than most suppose," Thoreau steers his way by "the faint track which I had worn" (117). After a snow storm, "half an hour sufficed to obliterate the tracks of the last traveller" (180), thereby restoring his solitude. His own path "abetted" both movement and navigation: "The wind blew the oak leaves into my tracks, where they lodged, and by absorbing the rays of the sun melted the snow, and so not only made a dry bed for my feet, but in the night their dark line was my guide" (172). And even in the depth of winter, "my own deep tracks . . . were often filled with heaven's own blue" (179). At his most rhapsodic, Thoreau even uses the word *track* to suggest that each of us has his own celestial railway:

> God himself culminates in the present moment. . . . And we are enabled to apprehend at all what is sublime and noble only by the perpetual instilling and drenching of the reality that surrounds us. The universe constantly and obediently answers to our

conceptions; whether we travel fast or slow, the track is laid for us. (69)

When Thoreau offers his explanation for leaving the pond, however, he returns to the sense of a track or path as confining:

It is remarkable how easily and insensibly we fall into a particular route, and make a beaten track for ourselves. I had not lived there a week before my feet wore a path from my door to the pond-side, and though it is five or six years since I trod it, it is still distinct. . . . [H]ow deep the ruts of tradition and conformity! (217)

Another name for what concerns Thoreau here is *habit.* Sherman Paul has described the Walden experiment as "the labor of domesticating oneself for inspiration," and that process almost certainly entailed the development of certain habits—of daily writing, of careful observations, of purposeful austerity. We might also call this process, to evoke another railroad term, a kind of *training,* a word Thoreau himself uses: "To read well, that is, to read books in a true spirit, is a noble exercise. . . . It requires a training such as the athletes underwent" (72). *Walden* thus becomes a description of Thoreau's habits, a set of training exercises for living joyously and wide awake.

Thoreau's ambivalent uses of *track* and *path* suggest that he recognized the possibility of *over*training, of a habit's going stale and becoming a "beaten track" leading nowhere. When does a habit become disabling? That question is central to *Walden* and to Thoreau's decision to quit the pond. In *The Gay Science,* Nietzsche admitted to loving "brief habits." "But one day its time is up," he writes without the hint of regret.

That is what happens to me with dishes, ideas, human beings, cities, poems, music, doctrines, ways of arranging the day, and life styles.

Enduring habits I hate. I feel as if a tyrant had come near me. . . . I feel grateful to all my misery and bouts of sickness and everything about me that is imperfect, because this sort of thing leaves me with a hundred backdoors through which I can escape from enduring habits.

In Nietzsche's terms, the Walden stay was Thoreau's brief habit, abandoned when he felt the tyrant at his door. Taken together, his book and his return to Concord record the abiding tension he felt between his resistance to routine and his need for it. Nietzsche understood this dilemma:

> Most intolerable, to be sure, and the terrible par excellence would be for me a life entirely devoid of habits, a life that would demand perpetual improvisation. That would be my exile in Siberia.

For Thoreau, when every gesture becomes obliged to promise originality and metaphor, the static and literal reassert their appeal. If he left the woods at least in part because his own track had become a beaten one, because, as we now say, he needed a change, that track had also led him to Walden Pond, which he celebrates as "itself unchanged, the same water which my youthful eyes fell on." "All the change," he added, "is in me" (132).

And another problem: the path that Thoreau made through the woods, the one that others have kept open, was *Walden* itself, whose particular route generations of readers have followed. Thoreau feared that those readers would not break their own trails; he also worried that he would find himself stuck on the same one. By announcing "I had several more lives to live," he was challenging himself to find other Waldens. Unable to do so, he transformed that experience into a permanently marked path. To succeed, therefore, *Walden* has to strike a balance: it should guide its reader toward her own transformation without imposing Thoreau's particular response to the question of how to live. "I would not have anyone adopt *my* mode of living on any account," he declares. "I would have each one be very careful to find out and pursue his *own* way" (52). But to the extent that *Walden* persuades us, it offers a ready-made path, available for use, compellingly blazed through Concord's woods and, by implication, through life itself.

(with Paul Johnson, Robert McDonald, and Charles Meyer)

U

35.

UNEXPLORABLE

We need the tonic of wildness. . . . At the same time that we are
earnest to explore and learn all things. we require that all things be
mysterious and unexplorable, that land and sea be infinitely wild,
unsurveyed and unfathomed by us because unfathomable. We can
never have enough of Nature. . . . We need to witness out own limits transgressed, and some life pasturing freely where we can never
wander. (213)

This stirring passage, an inspiration for the twentieth century's
deep ecology movement, suggests Thoreau's ambivalence toward
science. Although he corresponded regularly with Harvard zoolo-
gist Louis Agassiz and joined the Boston Society of Natural History in 1850, Thoreau was always more interested in describing and
classifying phenomena than in explaining them. If he did not adopt
Wordsworth's repudiation of science ("We murder to dissect" [*Lyrical Ballads*, "The Tables Turned," l. 28]), he was perfectly capable of
describing "the eye of science" as "barren" (*J*, 1 November 1851) and
of declaring "I begin to see . . . objects only when I leave off understanding them" (*J*, 14 February 1851).

When championing renewable energy, *New York Times* columnist
Thomas Friedman is fond of saying that "nature is only chemistry,
biology, and physics." In the early nineteenth century, however, it
had been much more. Wordsworth's famous line "We feel that we
are greater than we know" (*The River Duddon*, 34.14) offers the perfect summary of romanticism, and it was nature that had prompted

those feelings. Could the natural world's power to prompt intuitions of immortality survive scientific analysis? That question shadows Thoreau's walks through Walden's woods.

Walden's answer occasionally involves a radical rejection of man: "We need to witness our own limits transgressed, and some life pasturing freely where we never wander" (213). The *Journal* often celebrates moments when human order recedes:

> Moonlight on Fair Haven Pond seen from the Cliffs. A sheeny lake in the midst of a boundless forest. . . . This light and this hour take the civilization all out of the landscape. (*J*, 5 September 1851)

In other places, Thoreau makes his antihumanism more explicit:

> No true and absolute account of things,—of the evening and the morning and all the phenomena between them,—but ever a petty reference to man, to society, aye, often to Christianity. What these things are when men are asleep. I come from the funeral of mankind to attend to a natural phenomenon. The so much greater significance of any fact—of sun and moon and stars—when not referred to man and his needs but viewed absolutely! Sounds that are wafted from over the confines of time. (*J*, 10 November 1851).

Despite this entry's sacramental tone, Thoreau was rarely sentimental about seeing "our own limits transgressed." While Wordsworth's accounts of such experiences, of "low breathings coming after me, and sounds/Of undistinguishable motion" (*The Prelude*, 1.322–23), often resemble gothic fiction, Thoreau's, more rooted in factual description, become realistically frightening. Although he composed the most famous of these passages while at the pond, he kept it, and its mood, out of *Walden*. In what would become part of *The Maine Woods*, he described his ascent of Ktaadn in apocalyptic language:

> This was an undone extremity of the globe. . . . It was, in fact, a cloud factory. . . . It was vast, Titanic, and such as man never inhabits. Some part of the beholder, even some vital part, seems to escape through the loose grating of his ribs as he ascends. He is more alone than you can ever imagine. There is less of substantial

thought and fair understanding in him, than in the plains where men inhabit. His reason is dispersed and shadowy, more thin and subtle, like the air. Vast, Titanic, inhuman Nature has got him at disadvantage, caught him alone, and pilfers him of some of his divine faculty. She does not smile on him as in the plains. She seems to say sternly, why come ye here before your time? This ground is not prepared for you.

Even the uncompromising Thoreau must have realized that including too much of this kind of thing would have undermined even *Walden*'s slight commercial possibilities. But his ambivalence about such experiences, their capacity both to terrify and inspire, informs *Walden*.

Theodor Adorno once rejected a proposal from Walter Benjamin with a by-now famous admonition: "Your study is located at the crossroads of magic and positivism. That spot is bewitched. Only theory could break the spell." Divided between science and poetry, Thoreau took up residence at that same crossroads, but as the passage from "Spring" suggests, he did not want a cure: he preferred to remain spellbound. Indeed, during *Walden*'s revisions, he had already begun to lament the magic's dissipation:

I fear that the character of my knowledge is from year to year becoming more distinct and scientific—That in exchange for views as wide as heaven's cope I am being narrowed down to the field of the microscope. I see details, not wholes nor the shadow of the whole. (J, 19 August 1851)

The next day, however, as Sharon Cameron points out, Thoreau renewed his brief for science, admiring the precision of botanical language and longing for its equivalent to describe human sentiments and morals.

It's an uneasy truce, and *Walden* alternates between near-clinical recording and rhapsodic flights. In doing so, it suggests another of Thoreau's ambitions. For if "we require that all things be mysterious and unexplorable," that standard must apply to *Walden* itself. How could Thoreau produce a readable book that would also be "mysterious and unexplorable"? Susan Sontag once observed that with the removal of its caption, any photograph becomes art. At some point,

Thoreau seems to have made a similar discovery: remote from their original contexts, the simplest factual descriptions—a pond's exact depth, a winter's first freeze—get transformed into literature:

> It is surprising how any reminiscence of a different season of the year affects us. When I meet with any such in my Journal, it affects me as poetry. . . . You only need to make a faithful record of an average summer day's experience and summer mood, and read it in the winter, and it will carry you back to more than that summer day alone could show. (*J*, 26 October 1853)

This effect appears regularly in the *Journal*, where long philosophical passages abruptly shift gears. Thus, a discussion of the *Week* ends with a sentence resembling a note from *The Farmer's Almanac*:

> I thought that one peculiarity of my "Week" was its *hypaethral* character, to use an epithet applied to those Egyptian temples which are open to the heavens above, *under the ether.* I thought that it had little of the atmosphere of the house about it, but might wholly have been written, as in fact it was to a considerable extent, out-of-doors. It was only at a late period in writing it, as it happened, that I used any phrases implying that I lived in a house or led a *domestic* life. I trust it does not smell of the study and library, even of the poet's attic, as of the fields and woods; that it is a hypaethral or unroofed book, lying open under the ether and permeated by it, open to all weathers, not only to be kept on a shelf.
> The potatoes are beginning to blossom. (*J*, 29 June 1851)

Although this entry's first paragraph is the kind of writing popularly known as "Thoreauvian," the real Thoreau appears in the juxtaposition between that paragraph's argument and the six-word sentence that follows it: "The potatoes are beginning to blossom." Even one of his life's greatest days receives similar treatment:

> August 9. *Wednesday.*—To Boston.
> "Walden" published. Elder-berries. Waxwork yellowing. (*J*, 9 August 1854)

"Mere facts and names and dates communicate more than we suspect," Thoreau once noted (*J*, 27 January 1852). But they also communicate *less*, and their accumulation, especially in the long descriptions of *Walden*'s interior chapters, renders Thoreau's book "mysterious."

Ultimately, Thoreau cannot precisely define his experience in the woods; he can only say what it *felt* like. And even those feelings, eluding conventional description, can be represented only in atmospheric terms: "The true harvest of my daily life is something as intangible and indescribable as the tints of morning or evening. It is a little stardust caught, a segment of the rainbow which I have clutched" (147). As a result, for all the apparatus borrowed from the conventional essay, *Walden* is something different. Roland Barthes's description of his own autobiography perfectly suits Thoreau's book: "What replaces argumentation is the unfolding of an image." *Walden*'s image, now central to the American imagination, is of a man living beside a pond in a twelve-by-fifteen-foot cabin of his own making, with only the natural world around him for company. And despite all of Thoreau's meticulous annotations of that experience, this image, like *Walden* itself, remains inexhaustible, "mysterious and unexplorable."

(with Charles Meyer and Alex Washington)

36.

VOCATION

At various stages in his life, Thoreau earned his living as a school-teacher, lecturer, handyman (for Emerson), factory manager (for his family's pencil business), industrial designer (of the family pencils), tutor, and surveyor. "All men want . . . something to *do*, or rather something to *be*," he writes in *Walden* (19). But except for writing, which never provided him with anything like an adequate income, all regular occupations provoked in him a smothering anxiety. As early as 1841, when he was not yet twenty-four, Thoreau was already treating conventional work as a kind of death: "Most who enter on any profession are doomed men. The world might as well sing a dirge over them forthwith" (*J*, 27 March 1841). "As long as possible live free and uncommitted" (60), *Walden* advises: or, in other words, don't sign any employment contracts. "I have thoroughly tried school-keeping," Thoreau writes, punning on his own name while at the same time acknowledging—a rare thing—that he has had any previous occupations, "and I lost my time into the bargain" (50). "I have tried trade," he continues; "but I found that it would take ten years to get under way in that, and that then I should probably be on my way to the devil" (51).

Thoreau had caught his contempt for ordinary vocations from Emerson, whose 1837 essay "The American Scholar" described their destructiveness: "The tradesman . . . is ridden by the routine of his craft. . . . The priest becomes a form; the attorney a statue-book; the mechanic a machine; the sailor a rope of the ship." As he entered his mid-twenties, still without what his neighbors would have recognized as a regular job, Thoreau began to suggest something new: that a man's choice of occupation could result not only from an active interest in something but also from a revulsion prompted by mundane work. In a letter to Harrison Blake, written from Walden, Thoreau turns this revulsion into a challenge:

> I know many men who, in common things, are not to be deceived; who trust no moonshine; who count their money correctly, and know how to invest it; who are said to be prudent and knowing; who yet will stand at a desk the greater part of their lives, as cashiers in banks, and glimmer and rust and finally go out there. If they *know* anything, what under the sun do they do that for?

Even in his often critical eulogy, Emerson acknowledged that Thoreau had been "never idle or self-indulgent." At his cabin, Thoreau was, in fact, tirelessly writing: a draft of the *Week,* the long essay on Thomas Carlyle, "Civil Disobedience," roughly half of *Walden,* the Ktaadn sections of what would become *The Maine Woods.* But he had anticipated the distinction expressed by Stephen Sondheim and James Lapine in *Sunday in the Park with George:* "Work is what you do for others[;] . . . art is what you do for yourself." By the fall of 1854, in "Life Without Principle," his most abrasive essay, Thoreau would turn this attitude into an existential test:

> Do not hire a man who does your work for money, but him who does it for love of it.
> It is remarkable that there are few men so well employed . . . but that a little money or fame would commonly buy them off from their present pursuit.

In modern terms, if winning the lottery would make you quit your job the next day, you're in the wrong line of work.

Having begun *Walden* as a response to his neighbors' "impertinent" inquiries about his "mode of life" (5), Thoreau uses the occasion to convey his own industry. "I have always endeavored to acquire strict business habits," he assures his listeners. "My purpose in going to Walden Pond was . . . to transact some private business with the fewest obstacles" (16–17). The meticulous bookkeeping that follows, with expenses detailed to the quarter cent, shore up this practical persona. But Concord businessmen would have found less to admire in the more poetic accounts of what Thoreau's "business" actually involved:

> So many autumn, ay, and winter days, spent outside the town, trying to hear what was in the wind, to hear and carry it express! I well-nigh sunk all my capital in it. . . . [O]r waiting at evening on the hill-tops for the sky to fall, that I might catch something. . . . I was self-appointed inspector of snow storms and rain storms, and did my duty faithfully; surveyor, if not of highways, then of forest paths and all across-lot routes, keeping them open. (15)

These "enterprises," to use *Walden*'s word, don't sound like work. At the pond, however, Thoreau was inventing his own profession, whose duties he spelled out in his journal:

> I go forth to make new demands on life. I wish to begin this summer well; to do something in it worthy of it and of me; to transcend my daily routine and that of my townsmen; to have my immortality now, that it be in the *quality* of my daily life. . . . May I gird myself to be a hunter of the beautiful, that naught escape me! . . . I am eager to report the glory of the universe. . . . It is reasonable that a man should be something worthier at the end of the year than he was at the beginning. (*J*, 15 March 1852)

It's a hard job, and it would take all his time.

(with Brenda Maxey-Billings)

W

37.

WITHOUT BOUNDS

I desire to speak somewhere without bounds. (218)

This mysterious remark, appearing in *Walden*'s great "Conclusion," evokes Thoreau's regular employment as the village surveyor. His book seems designed to enable our own staking out of things, coming complete with tools (compasses, rulers, dividers) and measurements: the number of rods separating Thoreau's cabin from the railroad tracks, the exact distance from his site to Concord, the width and depth of the pond, the acreage of neighboring farms and lakes. In "Where I Lived and What I Lived For," Thoreau makes punning use of his occupation by declaring "I have thus surveyed the country on every side within a dozen miles of where I live," including, in yet another pun, "each farmer's premises" (58). Quoting Cowper's "Verses Supposed to Be Written by Alexander Selkirk" (Defoe's model for Robinson Crusoe), Thoreau even supplies his own italics: "I am monarch of all I *survey*" (59).

Since Thoreau so often earned his living by marking his neighbors' property lines, what are we to make of his "desire to speak somewhere *without* bounds"? The wish resembles another Thoreauvian longing, also characteristically expressed in spatial terms: "I love a broad margin to my life" (79). The two remarks remind us that Thoreau seemed to experience almost every kind of externally imposed rule, custom, or schedule as an occasion for claustrophobia. In Emerson's words, "He was a protestant *à l'outrance*." Some of *Walden*'s best critics have argued that this reflexive resistance extended to language itself, which, indeed, he often treated as something that gets in the way of living: "It is not easy to write in a journal what interests us at any time," he once observed, "because to write it is not what interests us." Andrew Delbanco goes further, describing Thoreau as "ultimately a despiser of culture." "What Thoreau discovered," Delbanco continues, "was that language itself . . . made him feel dead because it subjected him to the worn and degraded inventions of other minds." Some evidence supports this position. In an 1857 letter, Thoreau seems to anticipate Flaubert's dread of merely reproducing the banalities catalogued in his *Dictionary of Received Ideas:*

> How shall we account for our pursuits if they are original? We get the language with which to describe our various lives out of a common mint.

Almost certainly, Thoreau's brief against society occasionally extended to language, inevitably a social, communal phenomenon. Hence the dilemma: he hates whatever he associates with mass values and taste, but language's ability to communicate depends on its being something we have in common.

How does this issue appear in *Walden*? The book represents an attempt to use everyday language in *uncommon* ways; Thoreau wants to make *our* language *his own.* If he entirely succeeded in doing so, we wouldn't understand him at all. But he remakes the vocabulary of business and economics, dragging those terms beyond their normal boundaries, endowing words like "cost" and "worth" and "capital" with new meanings. "The cost of a thing is the amount of what I will call life which is required to be exchanged for it" (24). "There are more secrets in my trade than in most men's" (15). "I turned my face more exclusively than ever to the woods. . . . I determined to go into business at once, and not wait to acquire the usual capital" (16). These are sentences trying to refresh the idiom we share.

Thoreau's attitude toward language has another, more radical aspect, the fear that, as Geoffrey O'Brien puts it, "meanings dull his senses." "I begin to see . . . objects only when I leave off understanding them" (*J*, 14 February 1851), Thoreau had written before completing *Walden*, recognizing the inadequacy of even our most rigorously obtained knowledge, which almost always involves a linguistic dimension. Thoreau felt acutely that words, as O'Brien puts it, "have the curious power to paralyze the senses. A culture which enshrines a particular linguistic formulation of truth is a zombie kingdom." Hence Thoreau's response, a call almost inexplicable for a writer who at first wanted to sell books: "Give me a sentence which no intelligence can understand" (*Week*, 151). This is the side of Thoreau that would celebrate overhearing the Maine Indians' native language, "a purely wild and primitive American sound, as much as the barking of a *chickaree*, and I could not understand a syllable of it."

O'Brien's version of Thoreau would locate him somewhere between the romanticism of Shelley ("the mind in creation is as a fading coal. . . . [W]hen composition begins, inspiration is already on the decline") and the postmodernism of Roland Barthes, who found in Japan, where he understood almost nothing, a blissful "exemption from meaning." But throughout *Walden*, Thoreau seems too much in love with language, both as a tool for waking his readers and for its own sake, to fit this picture. The nearly two-million-word *Journal* suggests that for Thoreau, living and language were inseparable: more than simply a medium for recording his experiences, writing became the means for his engagement with the world.

Thoreau's "desire to speak somewhere *without* bounds," however, almost certainly did contribute to the difficulty he felt in producing books. He found the his journal's discrete entries more congenial than a book's requisite architecture, proposing, in his characteristic vocabulary, that books "must themselves be the unconstrained and natural harvest of their author's lives" (*Week*, 98). In January 1852, while working on yet another *Walden* draft, he confessed his doubts about longer forms:

> I do not know but thoughts written down thus in a journal might be printed in the same form with greater advantage—than if the related ones were brought together into separate essays. They are now allied to life—& are seen by the reader not to be far-fetched. It is more simple—less artful—I feel that in the other case I should have no proper frame for my sketches. (*J*, 27 January 1852)

And a day later, he continued to fret:

Perhaps I can never find so good a setting for my thought as I shall thus have taken them out of. The crystal never sparkles more brightly than in the cavern. . . . Where also will you ever find the true cement for your thoughts? How will you ever rivet them together without leaving the marks of the file? (*J*, 28 January 1852)

If his journal represented Thoreau's way of "speaking without bounds," what advantages did it provide him? Why did those advantages get lost in longer forms? How can one negotiate between the helter-skelter immediacy of a journal and the rhetorical demands of a book? Thoreau's first response to this question was the *Week*, a storage bin for everything he had already written, filed under the ready-made headings of the days of the week. "Like a library of the shorter works of Henry Thoreau," one biographer called it, and despite its intermittent pleasures, Thoreau did not manage to hide "the marks of the file."

Almost a century later, Wittgenstein would admit to the same difficulty:

If I am thinking about a topic just for myself and not with a view to writing a book, I jump about all round it; that is the only way of thinking that comes naturally to me. Forcing my thoughts into an ordered sequence is a torment for me.

Like Nietzsche, Wittgenstein solved this problem by turning his books into collections of fragments. Why didn't Thoreau choose that method for *Walden*? What would the book be like if he had? Simply a transcription of his journal entries?

Wittgenstein's own philosophy turned on the issue of boundaries, with the *Tractatus* attempting to draw the line between factual propositions, which can be meaningfully said, and metaphysical assertions, which can only be *shown*. Since "the sense of the world must lie outside the world," we cannot speak it, but Wittgenstein admired the impulse to try to:

All I wanted to do . . . was just *to go beyond* the world and that is to say beyond significant language. My whole tendency and I believe the tendency of all men who ever tried to write or talk Ethics or

Religion was to run against the boundaries of language. This running against the walls of our cage is perfectly, absolutely hopeless. Ethics so far as it springs from the desire to say something about the ultimate meaning of life, the absolute good, the absolute valuable, can be no science. What it says does not add to our knowledge in any sense. But it is a document of a tendency in the human mind which I personally cannot help respecting deeply and I would not for my life ridicule it.

Wittgenstein's "tendency in the human mind," the need to assert value, was Thoreau's first impulse. And yet, if *Walden* survives in the popular imagination, it does so less as a statement of certain truths than as a *demonstration* of how to live a better life.

(with Brandon Neslund)

X MARKS WALDEN'S DEPTH

During the winter of 1846, Thoreau mapped Walden Pond, partly to disprove the local myth of its "bottomlessness." Lying on the ice and taking soundings with a small stone and cod line, Thoreau produced surprisingly accurate measurements that revealed the water's actual depth: 102 feet. He also observed what he calls "this remarkable coincidence," which he drew on a map, "that the line of greatest length intersected the line of greatest breadth *exactly* at the point of greatest depth" (195). After leaving the woods, Thoreau would caution himself against ready generalizations: "Let me not be in haste to detect the *universal law*; let me see more clearly a particular instance of it!" (J, 25 December 1851). But in "The Pond in Winter," he is quickly off to the races. Proud of his *X*, he begins to speculate:

> Who knows but this hint would conduct to the deepest part of the
> ocean as well as of a pond or puddle? Is not this the rule also for
> the height of mountains, regarded as the opposite of valleys? (195)

This question prompts a paleontological surmise worthy of Sherlock Holmes: "If we knew all the laws of Nature, we should need only one fact, or the description of one actual phenomenon, to infer all the particular results at that point" (195). And he can't stop there, darting off restlessly on one of *Walden*'s most obscure flights:

> What I have observed of the pond is no less true in ethics. It is the
> law of average. Such a rule of the two diameters not only guides us

toward the sun in the system and the heart in man, but draw lines through the length and breadth of the aggregate of a man's particular daily behaviors and waves of life into his coves and inlets, and where they intersect will be the height and depth of his character. Perhaps we need only to know how his shores trend and his adjacent country or circumstances, to infer his depths and concealed bottom. (196)

Even a reader sympathetic to Thoreau will probably lose patience with this passage, the result of an unchecked metaphor. But it is also characteristic of *Walden* and what makes the book so inspiring: Thoreau's consistent willingness to put pressure on every chance and coincidence he detects, trying to see where they might lead. "We should be blessed if we lived in the present always," he advises in "Spring," "and took advantage of every accident that befell us" (211). Having a particularly vivid reverie interrupted by Channing's visit, Thoreau offers one of *Walden*'s secrets: "Mem. There never is but one opportunity of a kind." In the *X* of the Pond's map, he has seen an "opportunity."

The French surrealists would base an entire movement on this way of working. In *Nadja*, André Breton would articulate the formula:

I intend to mention in the margin of the narrative I have yet to relate, only the most decisive episodes of my life *as I can conceive it apart from its organic plan,* and only insofar as it is at the mercy of chance . . . temporarily escaping my control, admitting me to an almost forbidden world of sudden parallels, petrifying coincidences . . . flashes of light that would make you see, really *see,* if only they were not so much quicker than all the rest. I am concerned with facts of quite unverifiable intrinsic value, but which, by their absolutely unexpected, violently fortuitous character, and the kind of associations of suspect ideas they provoke . . . I am concerned, I say, with facts which may belong to the order of pure observation, but which on each occasion present all the appearances of a signal, without our being able to say precisely which signal, and of what.

Thoreau had been there before, speaking the same urgent language:

I saw the sun falling on a distant white pine wood. . . . It was like looking into dreamland. It is one of the avenues to my future. Certain coincidences like this are accompanied by a certain flash as of hazy lightning, flooding all the world with a tremulous serene light which it is difficult to see long at a time. (*J*, 21 November 1850).

Breton's method depended on a readiness to exploit what he described as "certain juxtapositions, certain combinations of circumstances which greatly surpass our understanding." For Thoreau, this response was almost always activated by nature:

Whole weeks or months of my summer life slide away in thin volumes like mist or smoke, till at length some warm morning, perchance, I see a sheet of mist blown down the brook to the swamp, its shadow flitting across the fields, which have caught a new significance from that accident; as that vapor is raised above the earth, so shall the next weeks be elevated above the plane of the actual. (*J*, 29 December 1841)

Walden's reputation, as well as its most quoted passages, largely derives from its first two chapters, especially "Economy," where Thoreau's "simplicity" lesson preaches that we can expand our lives by minimizing our needs. "Reduce the denominator," Thomas Carlyle had advised in *Sartor Resartus*, using the metaphor of division to represent life's fraction. Having written a sympathetic account of Carlyle's work, Thoreau knew and embraced that lesson. But *Walden* is also a record of *X*, Thoreau's eagerness to *multiply* life's possibilities by engaging intensely with every moment presented to him, to treat as sacred the geometry of chance. Even the coincidence of a pond's depth occurring at the intersection of two diameters becomes worth pursuing, like every accident that befalls us.

(with Adam Nikolaidis)

Y

39.

YEARS

Although Thoreau offers *Walden* as a straightforward account of his twenty-six-month sojourn in the woods from 4 July 1845 until 6 September 1847, the book was, in fact, as Robert Sattelmeyer observes, "the product of a long gestation." Thoreau almost certainly wrote most of the first two chapters, "Economy" and "Where I Lived and What I Lived For," at the pond, but he was still revising the seventh draft in 1854, the year of *Walden*'s publication. Thoreau's cut-and-paste habit of constructing essays and books out of his own journal, which he raided relentlessly, also insured that *Walden* would include material from years long *before* his retreat. The result is a complex palimpsest reflecting Thoreau's shifting attitudes over a period much longer than two years. In Sattelmeyer's words, "The book evolved along with the author until it became less a simple history of his life at Walden . . . and more the sum of his histories simultaneously present in the text." The obvious parallel lies with Wordsworth's *Prelude*, begun in 1799 but only published posthumously in 1850, the kind of work where revision merges with autobiography, becoming the means of self-discovery.

Textual scholars have convincingly argued that *Walden* benefited from Thoreau's resulting inability to find a ready publisher: forced to sit on his second book for almost seven years, Thoreau used the time to make it longer and better. Inevitably, however, that process, when combined with Thoreau's use of material from his journal, resulted in a work made up of parts composed at different times and places. *Walden*, in effect, anticipates filmmaking's readiness to build a continuous narrative out of discontinuous fragments. To render that process invisible, commercial cinema developed the protocols known as "continuity," with "matching" becoming its most important principle: the noticeable seam joining two shots gets hidden by graphic similarities, continuing action, connecting glances, common sounds, or consistent appearances—if Cary Grant is clean-shaven when he looks at Ingrid Bergman, he should not have a beard when she looks back.

It didn't take the word processor to teach authors that books don't have to be written in sequence. As a technology, writing enables discontinuous composition and endless revision. But essayists and novelists have shared the cinema's need for continuity, a means of making something of varied provenance seem all of one sustained piece. Inconsistencies born of a writer's intermittent attention (a character described as an only child suddenly acquiring siblings, Dr. Watson's wound alternating between leg and shoulder) threaten a novel's realistic spell, just as radical shifts in tone can undermine an essay's credibility.

Walden's retrospective mode confirms Wordsworth's maxim that art "takes its origin from emotion recollected in tranquility." Thoreau's willingness to mix descriptions and thoughts from different periods of his life also reflects another of Wordsworth's most famous directives: "Our continued influxes of feeling are modified and directed by our thoughts, which are indeed the representatives of our past feelings." Thoreau, in other words, will not confine himself to telling us only what he felt while he was actually at the pond; that experience becomes a magnet, attracting to itself everything that he has read, seen, thought, and lived during his entire life. As Robert Frost said admiringly of *Walden*,

A man may write well and very well all his life, yet only once in a lifetime have such luck with him in the choice of a subject—a real gatherer, to which everything in him comes tumbling. Thoreau's immortality may hang by a single book, but the book includes even his writing that is *not* in it. Nothing he ever said but sounds like a quotation from it. Think of the success of a man's pulling himself together under one one-word title. Enviable!

For the most part, *Walden* maintains a casual continuity, however digressive. The cracks appear in the mismatches of tense and reference. Offering itself as a history, *Walden* begins conventionally with the past tense: "When I wrote the following pages, or rather the bulk of them, I lived alone in the woods, a mile from any neighbor, in a house which I had built myself, on the shore of Walden Pond, in Concord, Massachusetts, and earned my living by the labor of my hands only" (5); "I turned my face more exclusively than ever to the woods" (17); "I borrowed an axe" (31); "I took up my abode" (61)—the narrative continues for three chapters. "Sounds," however, offers an abrupt shift: "As I sit at my window this summer afternoon, hawks are circling about my clearing" (81). A few pages later, more restless tenses collide: a paragraph that begins in the present, "Now that the cars are gone by and all the restless world with them . . . I am more alone than ever" (87), gives way to another, opening with the line, "Sometimes I heard the bells . . . when the wind was favorable" (86). In next chapter, "Solitude," the present tense reemerges: "This is a delicious evening," Thoreau announces. "I come and go with a strange liberty in Nature. . . . [I]t is as solitary where I live as on the prairies" (90–91). Since we associate the past tense and past imperfective with historical narration and storytelling, Thoreau's resort to the present, while surely the product of raiding an entry from his journal, also implies immediacy, the temporary elimination of the layers effected by recollection. For a brief moment, at least, the reader is back at the pond with Thoreau.

In other places, *Walden*'s "continuity errors" contradict Thoreau's claim to have written "the following pages, or rather the bulk of them," during his twenty-six months in the woods while also revealing how often he returned. "But the pond has risen steadily for two years," he records in a later chapter, "and now in the summer of '52 is just five feet higher than when I lived there" (124). "House-Warming" records the exact dates of Walden's complete freeze for every year from 1845 through 1853. "One pleasant morning after a cold night, February 24th, 1850" (202), he begins his account of striking the ice to make it boom. In passages like these, as William E. Cain notes, Thoreau's "shifts in chronology are sometimes startling, all the more so because he appears unfazed by them."

What is their effect on us? Only the fully attentive, the wholly *awake* reader will notice them. Did Thoreau leave them there to call us to occasional attention? Or did he simply wish to abide by his own principle, announced on *Walden*'s first page: "I, on my side, require of every writer, first or last, a simple and sincere account of his own life" (5)? Thoreau's life revolved around writing, and *Walden*'s mismatches provide a glimpse into that activity: the long struggle to bring his raw material into publishable form, the fits-and-starts composing, the many years of note taking and observation, the willingness to remain on watch.

(with Veronica Jordan)

Z

40.

ZANZIBAR

It is not worth the while to go round the world to count the cats in Zanzibar. Yet do this even until you can do better, and you may perhaps find some "Symmes' Hole" by which to get at the inside at last. . . . Explore thyself. Herein are demanded the eye and the nerve. Only the defeated and deserters go to the wars, cowards that run away and enlist. (216)

Thoreau's concept of *worth* is simultaneously intriguing and inconsistent. Although he rejects meaningless tasks like counting the cats in Zanzibar, he spent his own time carefully cataloguing every apple in Massachusetts, detailing Walden's rich organic life, and measuring the pond's exact depth. And, of course, he also knew about Zanzibar, which clearly stands for an exotic world rejected by Thoreau, but one *that tempted him*—note the contradiction here: he can only dismiss "Zanzibar" because he had been reading about it (in Charles Pickering's 1851 *The Races of Man*). Thoreau regularly returned to travel books, finally limiting himself to one a week, a constraint suggesting an addiction ("I read one or two shallow books of travel in the intervals of my work, till that employment made me ashamed of myself, and I asked where it was then that *I* lived" [71]).

This contradiction provokes curiosity about Thoreau's values. He partially reconciles his own inconsistency by advising, in preacher's diction, "yet do this even till you can do better, and you may perhaps find some 'Symmes' Hole' by which to get at the inside at last." What is the lesson here? That, in Wallace Stevens's phrase, "description is

revelation"? That even relatively mundane occupations, if purpose-
fully and honestly pursued, can *lead to* revelation? But don't these
conclusions simply reintroduce the question of worth? Doesn't
Walden have as one of its central purposes the goal of distinguishing among everyday tasks, classifying some as possible first steps
towards self-discovery and others as hopeless wastes of time?

The passage's context—the repudiation of the exotic in favor of
the everyday ("Explore thyself. Herein are demanded the eye and the
nerve. Only the defeated and deserters go to the wars, cowards who
run away and enlist") accompanied by the insistence that the true
explorer sails inward—recognizes that the tools necessary for self-
knowledge (ambition, dedication, discipline) can develop in such
routine work as measuring and recording the facts of nature, including the number of cats in Zanzibar. Hence the consoling words: "Yet
do this even till you can do better." This advice indicates that Thoreau
regarded *Walden* as a training manual, designed to demonstrate how
a reconceived everyday life might serve our most elevated desires.
Thus, "do this even till you can do better" preaches not to the sinner
but to the beginner: practice these scales, Thoreau seems to say, and
you will be able to play celestial music.

> I learned this, at least, by my experiment, that if one advances con-
> fidently in the direction of his dreams, and endeavors to live the
> life which he has imagined, he will meet with a success unexpected
> in common hours. (217)
>
> *(with Hanif Ali)*

NOTES

INTRODUCTION

I am quoting an account of the 1991 Modern Language Association survey provided in Lawrence Buell, *The Environmental Imagination* (Cambridge: Harvard University Press, 1995), 9. Stephen Fender also cites this poll in his introduction to *Walden* (Oxford: Oxford University Press, 1997), xxii. In saying that *Walden* "will find a home," I am echoing the glorious concluding words of Emerson's eulogy for Thoreau, reprinted in *Walden, Civil Disobedience, and Other Writings*, 3rd ed., ed. William Rossi (New York: Norton, 2008), 409: "Wherever there is knowledge, wherever there is virtue, wherever there is beauty, he will find a home."

"'Bivouacked' at his cabin" appears in William E. Cain, "Henry David Thoreau, 1817–1862: A Brief Biography," in *A Historical Guide to Henry David Thoreau*, ed. William E. Cain (Oxford: Oxford University Press, 2000), 35. Cain is quoting Thoreau's friend F. B. Sanborn. Wittgenstein's "Anything that I might reach by climbing a ladder does not interest me" appears in his *Culture and Value*, trans. Peter Winch (Chicago: University of Chicago Press, 1980), 7. Robert Richardson's "Read this book" is a blurb on the back of *Walden* (Boston: Beacon Press, 1997). Wittgenstein's simile of a man trapped in a room with dummy doors is recalled by D. A. T. Gasking and A. C. Jackson, "Wittgenstein as a Teacher," in *Ludwig Wittgenstein: The Man and His Philosophy*, ed. K. T. Fann (Atlantic Highlands, N.J.: Humanities Press, 1967), 52. On Thoreau's attitude toward money, see Robert Louis Stevenson's "Henry David Thoreau," in his *Selected Essays* (Chicago: Regnery, 1959), 140–41:

> The point is the sanity of his view of life, and the insight with which
> he recognized the position of money, and thought out for himself the
> problem of riches and a livelihood. Apart from his eccentricities, he
> had perceived, and was acting on, a truth of universal application. For

money enters in two different characters into the scheme of life. A certain amount, varying with the number and empire of our desires, is a true necessary to each one of us in the present order of society; but beyond that amount, money is a commodity to be bought or not to be bought, a luxury in which we may either indulge or stint ourselves, like any other.

Ronald B. Schwartz's remark appears in his essay "Private Discourse in Thoreau's *Walden*," in *Henry David Thoreau's "Walden*," ed. Harold Bloom (New York: Chelsea House, 1987), 79. Stanley Cavell, *The Senses of Walden* (San Francisco: North Point, 1981), 20, comments tellingly on Thoreau's "An old-fashioned man would have lost his senses or died of ennui." Roland Barthes's call for "an interrogative reading" appears in his essay "The Third Meaning," in *The Responsibility of Forms*, trans. Richard Howard (New York: Hill and Wang, 1985), 43. For a powerful indictment of contemporary literary studies, see Mark Edmundson, "Against Readings," *Chronicle of Higher Education*, 24 April 2009, B7–10. For a longer discussion of these issues, and one particularly appropriate to *Walden's* concerns, see Anthony T. Kronman, *Education's End: Why Our Colleges and Universities Have Given Up on the Meaning of Life* (New Haven: Yale University Press, 2007).

For my previous use of the ABCs method, see *The ABCs of Classic Hollywood* (Oxford: Oxford University Press, 2008). Krutch's remark appears in his *Henry David Thoreau* (New York: William Sloane, 1948), 120. Wittgenstein's comment about "seeing connections" appears in *Philosophical Investigations*, trans. G. E. M. Anscombe (Oxford, U.K.: Blackwell, 2001), 42. For Nietzsche's remark ("A book such as this is not for reading straight through"), see *Daybreak: Thoughts on the Prejudices of Morality*, trans. R. J. Hollingdale (Cambridge: Cambridge University Press, 1982), 457. Wittgenstein's remark about doing everything twice appears in *Wittgenstein's Lectures: Cambridge, 1930–1932*, ed. Desmond Lee (Oxford, U.K.: Blackwell, 1980), 24. The tour guide metaphor is cited in Gasking and Jackson, "Wittgenstein as a Teacher," 51.

1. ADVENTURE

Jean-Paul Sartre, *Nausea*, trans. Lloyd Alexander (New York: New Directions, 1964), 39. For Nietzsche's remark about adventurers and surveyors, see *Human, All Too Human*, trans. Marion Faber and Stephen Lehmann (London: Penguin, 1984), 10.

2. ANTS

Thoreau, of course, did not entirely cut himself off from news, family, and neighbors; he readily admits that "I walked in the village to see the men and boys" (115). But even that chapter, presumably devoted to those excursions, dismisses the town gossips and spends far more time on the experience of getting lost in the woods as he returned to his cabin in the dark. Epstein's remark appears in "The Senses 1 (b)," in *French Film Theory and Criticism, 1907–1939*, 2 vols., ed. Richard Abel (Princeton: Princeton University Press, 1988), 1:242.

3. AWAKE

Thoreau's self-description ("I am a mystic") originated as part of his response to a questionnaire from the Association for the Advancement of Science. See Robert Richardson, *Henry Thoreau: A Life of the Mind* (Berkeley: University of California Press, 1986), 285. Stephen Fender's essay on Thoreau constitutes his introduction to the Oxford World Classics edition of *Walden* (Oxford: Oxford University Press, 1997). While many critics have discussed Thoreau's habitual punning and remotivations of *Walden*'s most important words, I have found two writers especially useful on this point: Stanley Cavell, *The Senses of Walden* (San Francisco: North Point, 1981), and Judith P. Saunders, "Economic Metaphor Redefined: The Transcendentalist Capitalist at Walden," in *Henry David Thoreau's "Walden,"* ed. Harold Bloom (New York: Chelsea House, 1987), 59–67. Commenting on Thoreau's inherited sleeping sickness, Richardson observes that "this affliction adds a sly and touching twist to Thoreau's repeated use of wakefulness as a metaphor for consciousness and spiritual life" (126). On Thoreau's "being interested," see Richardson, 376: "Thoreau's nearly limitless capacity for being interested is one of the most unusual and attractive things about him." The Wallace Stevens lines from "Notes toward a Supreme Fiction" are in *Collected Poems* (New York: Vintage, 1982), 386.

4. BASKETS

For a book-length discussion of Thoreau's attempts to make a living from his writing, see Steven Fink, *Prophet in the Marketplace: Thoreau's Development as a Professional Writer* (Columbus: Ohio State University Press, 1999). The critic describing the *Week* as "a commercial disaster" is Gary Scharnhorst, *Henry David Thoreau: A Case Study in Canonization* (Columbia, S.C.: Camden House, 1993). I discovered this comment in William E. Cain, "Henry David Thoreau, 1817–1862: A Brief Biography," in *A Historical Guide to Henry David Thoreau*, ed. William E. Cain (Oxford: Oxford University Press, 2000), 37. For a longer discussion of the gap between the introduction and acceptance of innovative work, see Robert B. Ray, "How to Start an Avant-Garde," in *How a Film Theory Got Lost and Other Mysteries in Cultural Studies* (Bloomington: Indiana University Press, 2001), 74–82. Stendhal's famous remark about being read in 1935 appears in *The Life of Henry Brulard*; I have taken it from a gloss in *Red and Black*, trans. Robert M. Adams (New York: Norton, 1969), 432.

Francis Haskell's "Enemies of Modern Art," in his *Past and Present in Art and Taste* (New Haven: Yale University Press, 1987), 207–33, is the most important discussion of this entry's topic and one to which I am greatly indebted. My discussion of the impressionists' maneuvers partially derives from the superb book by Harrison C. White and Cynthia A. White, *Canvases and Careers: Institutional Change in the French Painting World* (Chicago: University of Chicago Press, 1993). For a discussion of the bourgeois preference for "the licked surface," see Charles Rosen's and Henri Zerner's brilliant essay "The Ideology of the Licked Surface: Official Art," in their *Romanticism and Realism: The Mythology of Nineteenth-Century Art* (New York: Viking, 1984), 203–32.

Wordsworth's observation about the need for an innovative artist to create "the taste by which he is to be enjoyed" appears in his 1815 "Essay, Supplementary to the Preface," reprinted in his *Selected Prose*, ed. John O. Hayden (New York: Penguin, 1988), 408. For Baudelaire's influential art criticism, see *The Painter of Modern Life and Other Essays*, ed. Jonathan Mayne (New York: Phaidon, 1964). The leading discussion of Thoreau's quarrel with transcendentalism can be found in Joel Porte, *Emerson and Thoreau: Transcendentalists in Conflict* (Middletown: Wesleyan University Press, 1966). Equally useful on this point is Sharon Cameron's *Writing Nature: Henry Thoreau's Journal* (Chicago: University of Chicago Press, 1985). In his introduction to the Oxford World's Classics edition of *Walden* (Oxford: Oxford University Press, 1997), Stephen Fender reports that "a recent survey of American professors found that they considered *Walden* by far the most important nineteenth-century text to teach to their students—well ahead of *The Scarlet Letter* and *Moby Dick*" (xxii).

5. BOOKS

"Manifesto of transcendentalism" comes from Robert Richardson, *Henry Thoreau: A Life of the Mind* (Berkeley: University of California Press, 1986), 21. For Thoreau's attitude toward fiction, see his comment, "I never read a novel, they have so little real life and thought in them," cited by Norman Foerster, "The Intellectual Heritage of Thoreau," in *Twentieth Century Interpretations of Walden*, ed. Richard Ruland (Englewood Cliffs, N.J.: Prentice-Hall, 1969), 48. Emerson's comments about Thoreau appear in his eulogy, now simply known as "Thoreau," found in most collections of Emerson's writings, as well as in *Walden, Civil Disobedience, and Other Writings*, 3rd ed., ed. William Rossi (New York: Norton, 2008), 394–409. Richardson, *Henry Thoreau*, 54–57, usefully discusses the New England interest in "self-culture." Alcott's remark about the inappropriateness of Emerson's eulogy is quoted by Robert Sattelmeyer, "Thoreau and Emerson," in *The Cambridge Companion to Henry David Thoreau*, ed. Joel Myerson (Cambridge: Cambridge University Press, 1995), 36. Sattelmeyer provides an especially useful account of Thoreau's Oedipal struggle with Emerson, one that complements

Joel Porte, *Emerson and Thoreau: Transcendentalists in Conflict* (Middletown: Wesleyan University Press, 1966). Wittgenstein's remarks on aspect and aspect blindness come from *Philosophical Investigations*, trans. G. E. M. Anscombe (Oxford, U. K.: Blackwell, 2001), 165, 182. His remark about a philosopher's search for "the liberating word" appears in what is known as *The Big Typescript*, but it can be more readily found in *The Wittgenstein Reader*, 2nd ed., ed. Anthony Kenny (Oxford, U.K.: Blackwell, 2006), 47.

6. COLORS

Wittgenstein's "Colours spur us to philosophize" is quoted in Ray Monk, *Ludwig Wittgenstein: The Duty of Genius* (New York: Penguin, 1990), 561. Thoreau's response to Virgil, "It was the same world," is cited in Robert Richardson, *Henry Thoreau: A Life of the Mind* (Berkeley: University of Chicago Press, 1986), 25. On Wittgenstein's use of color words, see Severin Schroeder, *Wittgenstein* (Cambridge, U.K.: Polity, 2006), 177.

7. DEATH

"I put the best face on the matter," a remark Thoreau removed from *Walden,* is quoted by Robert Sattelmeyer, "The Remaking of *Walden*," in *Walden, Civil Disobedience, and Other Writings,* 3rd ed., ed. William Rossi (New York: Norton, 2008), 501. For Geoffrey O'Brien's comment on the passage from the *Week,* see his "Thoreau's Book of Life," *New York Review of Books,* 15 January 1987, 47. Samuel Johnson's famous remark appears in James Boswell, *The Life of Samuel Johnson* (New York: Knopf, 1992), 748. Wallace Stevens's line is from his poem "Sunday Morning," in *Collected Poems* (New York: Vintage, 1982), 69.

8. DISTANCE

Cavell's "The problem is his right to declare it" appears in *The Senses of Walden* (San Francisco: North Point, 1981), 11. For Wittgenstein's "If you want to go deep down," see his *Culture and Value,* trans. Peter Winch (Chicago: University of Chicago Press, 1980), 50e. I have taken the information about the paucity of Concord residents who lived alone from Robert A. Gross, "'That Terrible Thoreau': Concord and Its Hermit," in *A Historical Guide to Henry David Thoreau,* ed. William E. Cain (Oxford: Oxford University Press, 2000), 186: "Hardly anybody in Concord lived alone. In 1850, just three years after Thoreau's sojourn at Walden, the census-taker found only thirteen individuals, in a town of 2,249, keeping house on their own, apart from family and friends. Nearly all were women: old, poor widows and spinsters, without anybody to care for them. Their isolation constitutes a cruel necessity, not a philosophical choice." Geoffrey O'Brien's comment, "You begin by reading a book and find that you have crossed over into a life,"

appears in his essay "Thoreau's Book of Life," *New York Review of Books,*
15 January 1987, 46. Thoreau's remark, "I never read a novel," is quoted by
Norman Foerster, "The Intellectual Heritage of Thoreau," in *Twentieth Century Interpretations of Walden,* ed. Richard Ruland (Englewood Cliffs, N.J.:
Prentice-Hall, 1968), 48.

9. DRUMMER

Hawthorne's comment is cited by Leon Edel, *Henry David Thoreau* (Minneapolis: University of Minnesota Press, 1970), 28. For Emerson's comments
on Thoreau, including the remark about "a huckleberry party," see "Thoreau" in *Walden, Civil Disobedience, and Other Writings,* 3rd ed., ed. William Rossi (New York: Norton, 2008), 407. Lowell's "Thoreau" is reprinted
in this same volume, and his dismissive remark about "the state of his personal thermometer" appears on 417. For James's remark, see his *Essays on
Literature: American Writers, English Writers* (New York: Library of America, 1984), 265, 391–92. Stevenson's comments about Thoreau come from
his essay "Henry David Thoreau," in his *Selected Essays* (Chicago: Regnery,
1959), 129, 131–32, 134, 147. In a note on Thoreau's insistence that "I would
not have any one adopt my mode of living," Walter Harding comments, "It
is important to call attention to this line, for so many ask, 'What if everyone
lived like T?'" (*Walden: An Annotated Edition,* ed. Walter Harding [Boston:
Houghton Mifflin, 1995], 68). Pascal's diagnosis of "all man's unhappiness"
appears in *Pensées,* ed. Louis Lafuma (Paris: Delmas, 1948), frag. 136. For
Voltaire's comments on Pascal, see *The Works of Voltaire,* vol. 21, trans. William F. Fleming (Paris: DuMont, 1901), 234. Nietzsche's description of "free-
spirited people" appears in *Human, All Too Human,* trans. Marion Faber and
Stephen Lehmann (London: Penguin, 1984), 173–74. Nietzsche's "The greatest danger" appears in *The Gay Science,* trans. Walter Kaufmann (New York:
Vintage, 1974), 130–31.

10. EXPERIMENT

William E. Cain's characterization of Thoreau's Walden stay as "bivouack-
ing" cites Thoreau's friend F. B. Sanborn as the source in "Henry David Thoreau, 1817–1862: A Brief Biography," in *A Historical Guide to Henry David
Thoreau,* ed. William E. Cain (Oxford: Oxford University Press, 2000), 35.
For Thoreau's letter to Blake about his reluctance to give up a winter for lecturing, see Henry David Thoreau, *Letters to a Spiritual Seeker,* ed. Bradley P.
Dean (New York: Norton, 2004), 145. The remark about the choice of vocation as "a grave question" appears on 41 of the same book. For Sherman Paul's
astute diagnosis of Thoreau's vocational problems, see *The Shores of America: Thoreau's Inward Exploration* (Urbana: University of Illinois Press, 1972),
16, 21. Emerson's "Literary Ethics" lecture is included in *Emerson: Essays and
Poems* (New York: Library of America, 1996), 111. Carlyle's famous sentence,

"The Fraction of Life can be increased in value not so much by increasing your Numerator as by lessening your Denominator," appears in the chapter "The Everlasting Yea" in his *Sartor Resartus* (London: Chapman and Hall, 1831), 132. On experimenting, see Daniel S. Milo, "Towards an Experimental History of Gay Science," *Strategies* 4/5 (1991): 90–91. Stephen Fender's introduction to the Oxford World Classics 1997 edition of *Walden* has a useful discussion of the self-help literature that surrounded *Walden*. Fender also points out the hopelessness of Thoreau's accounts and the futility of his farming. Breton's dismissal of work appears in his *Nadja,* trans. Richard Howard (New York: Grove, 1960), 60. Geoffrey O'Brien's "Thoreau's Book of Life" appears in the *New York Review of Books*, 15 January 1987, 46–51. See esp. 46.

11. FASHION

Loos's "Ornament and Crime" is included in Ulrich Conrads, ed., *Programs and Manifestoes on 20th-Century Architecture* (Cambridge: MIT Press, 1971), 19–24. The quoted passages are from 20, 22, 24, and 19. For a useful discussion of Loos's essay, see Miriam Gusevich, "Decoration and Decorum, Adolf Loos's Critique of Kitsch," *New German Critique* 43 (Winter 1988): 97–123, and Peter Wollen, *Raiding the Icebox: Reflections on Twentieth-Century Culture* (Bloomington: Indiana University Press, 1993), 13–16. Astonishingly, when charged with pedophilia, Loos fled Vienna for Paris, where he designed a house for Josephine Baker.

Thoreau's eighty-five-word sentence, which ironically denounces the nation as "unwieldy and overgrown" while calling for "a rigid economy, a stern and more than Spartan simplicity," appears in "Where I Lived and What I Lived For" (66):

> The nation itself, with all its so called internal improvements, which by the way, are all external and superficial, is just such an unwieldy and overgrown establishment, cluttered with furniture and tripped up by its own traps, ruined by luxury and heedless expense, by want of calculation and a worthy aim, as the million households in the land; and the only cure for it as for them is in a rigid economy, a stern and more than Spartan simplicity of life and elevation of purpose.

On positivism, see Auguste Comte, *Introduction to Positive Philosophy,* trans. Frederick Ferré (Indianapolis, Ind.: Bobbs-Merrill, 1970). "The world is everything that is the case" is the first line of Wittgenstein's *Tractatus Logico-Philosophicus,* trans. C. K. Ogden (Minneola, N.Y.: Dover, 1999), 29. In his *Raiding the Icebox,* 39–40, Peter Wollen also associates the repudiation of ornament with the attack on metaphysics, made explicit by Rudolf Carnap's 1932 essay "The Elimination of Metaphysics through Logical Analysis of Language," a critique of Heidegger. Thoreau's remark about Confucius is cited by Joel Porte, *Emerson and Thoreau: Transcendentalists in Conflict* (Middletown: Wesleyan University Press, 1966), 112.

12. FLUTE

Caroline Moseley, "Henry D. Thoreau and His Favorite Popular Song," *Journal of Popular Culture* 12.4 (1979): 624. Moseley identifies "Tom Bowling" as Thoreau's favorite. A synthesizer rendition of that tune can be heard at www.psymon.com/walden/cong.html, a site that offers both the lyrics and sheet music for it. Susan Sontag's comment about taste appears in her "Notes on 'Camp,'" in *Against Interpretation* (New York: Delta, 1966), 276: "One of the facts to be reckoned with is that taste tends to develop very unevenly. It's rare that the same person has good visual taste and good taste in people and taste in ideas." For Wittgenstein's remark to Russell, see Ray Monk, *Ludwig Wittgenstein: The Duty of Genius* (London: Penguin, 1990), 65. For Burch's summary of Bresson's position, see Noël Burch, *Theory of Film Practice,* trans. Helen R. Lane (Princeton: Princeton University Press, 1981), 90. The live 23 January 1945 Furtwängler recording of Brahms is included on *Wilhelm Furtwängler Conducts Johannes Brahms,* Music and Arts CD-4941 (4). For Gilberto Perez's observation about sound, see his *The Material Ghost: Films and Their Medium* (Baltimore: Johns Hopkins University Press, 1998), 83.

13. FULL OF HOPE

Seymour Chatman's essay is reprinted in *Film Theory and Criticism,* ed. Leo Braudy and Marshall Cohen (New York: Oxford University Press, 1999), 435–51. Robert Richardson's remark about Thoreau's early scenic descriptions appears in his book *Henry Thoreau: A Life of the Mind* (Berkeley: University of California Press, 1986), 52. Richardson also describes Thoreau's winter moods, 310–11. T. S. Eliot defines "objective correlative" in "Hamlet," which appears in *Selected Essays* (New York: Harcourt, Brace and World, 1964), 124–25:

> The only way of expressing emotion in the form of art is by finding an "objective correlative"; in other words, a set of objects, a situation, a chain of events which shall be the formula of that *particular* emotion; such that when the external facts, which must terminate in sensory experience, are given, the emotion is immediately evoked.

Eliot's phrase "the verbal equivalent for states of mind and feeling" appears in his essay "The Metaphysical Poets," in *Selected Essays,* 248.

14. GENIUS

Emerson's remarks about Thoreau come from his eulogy, "Thoreau," reprinted in the *Walden, Civil Disobedience, and Other Writings,* 3rd ed., ed. William Rossi (New York: Norton, 2008), 405. Henry James's comments can be found in his book on Hawthorne, in his *Essays on Literature: American Writers, English Writers* (New York: Library of America, 1984), 391–92. For Stevenson's comments on Thoreau, see Robert Louis Stevenson, "Henry David Thoreau," in *Selected Essays* (Chicago: Regnery, 1959), 148. Andrew Delbanco suggests that Thoreau worked "as if he anticipated the new compositional possibilities that have become available to us all through the word processor" (*Required Reading: Why Our American Classics Matter Now* [New York: Farrar, Straus and Giroux, 1997], 37). Linck C. Johnson applies Samuel Johnson's criticism of Milton to Thoreau's *Week* in "A Week on the Concord and Merrimack Rivers," in *The Cambridge Companion to Henry David Thoreau,* ed. Joel Myerson (Cambridge: Cambridge University Press, 1995), 40.

15. GOOD AND EVIL

The opening Nietzsche quote comes from *The Gay Science,* trans. Walter Kaufmann (New York: Vintage, 1974), 79. For "Language is a lie," see Nietzsche's "On Truth and Lie in an Extra-Moral Sense," in *The Portable Nietzsche,* trans. Walter Kaufmann (New York: Viking, 1968), 42–47. Nietzsche's remarks about the Greeks, knowledge as a useful error, and God's death appear in *The Gay Science,* 38, 169, 181–82. For Thoreau's letter to Blake, see Henry David Thoreau, *Letters to a Spiritual Seeker,* ed. Bradley P. Dean (New York: Norton, 2004), 38.

16. HIGHER LAWS

For the letter to Harrison Blake cited here, see Henry David Thoreau, *Letters to a Spiritual Seeker,* ed. Bradley P. Dean (New York: Norton, 2004), 38.

17. IDLENESS

Channing's description of Thoreau's cabin as "a wooden inkstand" is quoted by Carlos Baker, *Emerson among the Eccentrics* (New York: Viking, 1996), 265. I have added the italics to the economic words in the *Walden* passages quoted. For a superb discussion of Thoreau's redefinition of these terms, see Judith P. Saunders, "Economic Metaphor Redefined: The Transcendental Capitalist at Walden," in *Henry David Thoreau's "Walden,"* ed. Harold Bloom (New York: Chelsea House, 1987), 59–67. Cavell cites Emerson's "nervous and wretched" response to reading Thoreau (*The Senses of Walden* [San Francisco: North Point, 1981], 12). His characterization of Thoreau's "drones of fact" appears on 16. Sharon Cameron's brilliant articulation of the significance-description opposition appears in her book *Writing Nature: Henry Thoreau's Journal* (Chicago: University of Chicago Press, 1985). I have discovered several of the *Journal* passages I cite in Cameron's book.

Barthes's remark that "description . . . has its spiritual equivalent in contemplation" appears in his *Empire of Signs,* trans. Richard Howard (New York: Hill and Wang, 1982), 78. On meaninglessness as "bliss," see Roland Barthes, *The Pleasure of the Text,* trans. Richard Miller (New York: Hill and Wang, 1975), 23. Barthes's discussion of Amiel appears in the same book, 53–54. The Fox Talbot discussion appears in Ian Jeffrey, *Photography: A Concise History* (New York: Oxford University Press, 1981), 12–13. On insignificant details as "a luxury," see Barthes, "The Reality Effect," in *The Rustle of Language,* trans. Richard Howard (New York: Hill and Wang, 1986), 141. Barthes's film stills discussion is "The Third Meaning," in *The Responsibility of Forms,* trans. Richard Howard (New York: Hill and Wang), 48–49, 55, 57. Bazin's essays appear in his *What Is Cinema?* 2 vols., trans. Hugh Gray (Berkeley: University of California Press, 1967–71), 1:9–16, 23–40. His call for "self-effacement" appears on 29. His praise for *The Bicycle Thieves* appears in *What Is Cinema?* 2:52. Thoreau's advice to express a fact "without expressing yourself" is cited by Robert Richardson, *Henry Thoreau: A Life of the Mind* (Berkeley: University of California Press, 1986), 251. I have had my attention called to *Walden*'s torpid snake by Stephen Fender's discussion in his introduction to the Oxford World's Classics edition of *Walden* (Oxford: Oxford University Press, 1997), xxxix–xl.

18. 4 JULY 1845

Stanley Cavell, *The Senses of Walden* (San Francisco: North Point, 1981), 8–9: "We know the specific day in the specific year on which all the ancestors of New England took up their abode in the woods. That moment of origin is the national event reenacted in the events of *Walden,* in order this time to do it right. . . . America exists only in its discovery and its discovery was always an accident." F. Scott Fitzgerald, *The Great Gatsby* (New York: Scribner, 1992), 152. Jeffrey S. Cramer's gloss on *Walden*'s discussion of "gala days" tells us that "Concord celebrated two gala days, the anniversary of the battle there on 19 April 1775 and Independence Day on the Fourth of July" (*Walden: A Fully Annotated Edition* [New Haven: Yale University Press, 2004], 154n37). Nietzsche's dissection of philanthropy, which greatly resembles Thoreau's, appears in *The Gay Science,* trans. Walter Kaufmann (New York: Vintage, 1974), 92:

> A man's virtues are called *good* depending on their probable consequences not for him but for us and society. . . . [V]irtues (like industriousness, obedience, chastity, filial piety, and justice) are usually harmful for those who possess them. . . . When you have a virtue, a real, whole virtue . . . you are its *victim.*

Joel Porte's comment appears in his book *Emerson and Thoreau: Transcendentalists in Conflict* (Middletown: Wesleyan University Press, 1966), 150.

19. KITTLYBENDERS

Emerson's remark, "Only the architect had unfortunately omitted the stairs," is quoted in Robert Milder, *Reimagining Thoreau* (Cambridge: Cambridge University Press, 1995), 62. For Emerson's use of "skating on thin ice," see Eric Partridge, *A Dictionary of Clichés*, 5th ed. (New York: Routledge, 1979), 203. The word count for Thoreau's *Journal* comes from *I to Myself: An Annotated Selection from the Journal of Henry D. Thoreau*, ed. Jeffrey S. Cramer (New Haven: Yale University Press, 2007), xv. Richardson's remark appears in his *Henry Thoreau: A Life of the Mind* (Berkeley: University of California Press, 1986), 325. Nietzsche's comments about approaching "deep problems like cold baths" comes from *The Gay Science*, trans. Walter Kaufmann (New York: Vintage, 1974), 343–44. Both Margaret Fuller's remark on Thoreau's work as "a mosaic" and Delbanco's description of Thoreau's use of "modular blocks" appear in Delbanco's *Required Reading: Why Our American Classics Matter Now* (New York: Farrar, Straus and Giroux, 1997), 37–38. Rilke's famous line is in his poem "Archaic Torso of Apollo." The Serres remark appears in Michel Serres and Bruno Latour, *Conversations on Science, Culture, and Time*, trans. Roxanne Lapidus (Ann Arbor: University of Michigan Press, 1995), 69. David Pears's description of Wittgenstein's compositional style appears in Brian Magee, *Modern British Philosophy* (New York: St. Martin's, 1971), 39. Nietzche's advice to "approach deep problems like cold baths" appears in *The Gay Science*, trans. Walter Kaufmann (New York: Vintage, 1974), 343–44.

20. LEAVING WALDEN

The 22 January 1852 *Journal* passage and the sentences from *Walden*'s manuscript ("I put the best face on the matter") are both quoted in Robert Sattelmeyer's superb essay "The Remaking of *Walden*," in *Walden, Civil Disobedience, and Other Writings*, 3rd ed., ed. William Rossi (New York: Norton, 2008), 497, 501. For a discussion of Heidegger's notion of mood, see Mark Wrathall, *How to Read Heidegger* (New York: Norton, 2006), 30–35. I have relied on Wrathall for my understanding of Heidegger's thinking on this point. For the notion of the gradual replacement of significance with description, see Sharon Cameron's invaluable book, *Writing Nature: Henry Thoreau's Journals* (Chicago: University of Chicago Press, 1985), esp. 5.

21. MOLTING

Thoreau's deleted remark ("I put the best face on the matter"), which appears in the manuscript of *Walden,* is quoted by Robert Sattelmeyer, "The Remaking of *Walden*," reprinted in *Walden, Civil Disobedience, and Other Writings,* 3rd. ed., ed. William Rossi (New York: Norton, 2008), 501. For Emerson's Dartmouth address, see *Emerson: Essays and Poems* (New York:

Library of America, 1996), 110–11. Emerson's eulogy for Thoreau is reprinted in *Walden, Civil Disobedience, and Other Writings*. The quoted passages appear on 395, 407.

22. NAME

On Thoreau's changing the order of his first two names, see Walter Harding, *The Days of Henry Thoreau* (Princeton: Princeton University Press, 1982), 54. William E. Cain also suggests that Thoreau may have taken this step "to affirm a measure of independence from his family and to signify the new person he had become" ("Henry David Thoreau, 1817–1862: A Brief Biography," in *A Historical Guide to Henry David Thoreau*, ed. William E. Cain [Oxford: Oxford University Press, 2000], 11). I found the remark from Thoreau's Harvard commencement address in Sherman Paul, *The Shores of America: Thoreau's Inward Exploration* (Urbana: University of Illinois Press, 1972), 48.

Wittgenstein's comments on his method appear in *Philosophical Investigations*, trans. G. E. M. Anscombe (Oxford, U.K.: Blackwell, 2001), 40e. Wittgenstein's comparison of his philosophy to rearranging a bookshelf appears in *The Blue and Brown Books* (New York: Harper Torchbooks, 1960), 44–45. His remark, "One of the greatest hindrances to philosophy," appears in *The Wittgenstein Reader*, 2nd ed., ed. Anthony Kenny (Oxford, U.K.: Blackwell, 2006), 53. Wittgenstein's comment that "we have only to put together in the right way what we *know*," is quoted in Marie McGinn, *Wittgenstein and the Philosophical Investigations* (London: Routledge, 1997), 22. "Since everything lies open" and "The aspects of things that are most important for us" come from *Philosophical Investigations*, 43e. His admission that "what we say will be easy, but to know why we say it will be very difficult," can be found in *Wittgenstein's Lectures: Cambridge, 1932–1935*, ed. Alice Ambrose (Amherst, N.Y.: Prometheus, 2001), 77. The language game involving the tribe of builders appears in Wittgenstein's *Philosophical Investigations*, 3e.

23. NUMBERS

I have gathered most of these numbers from Walter Harding's useful notes to *Walden: An Annotated Edition*, ed. Walter Harding (Boston: Houghton Mifflin, 1993).

24. OBSCURITY

Mallarmé's remark ("Attendez, par pudeur . . . que j'y ajoute, du moins, un peu d'obscurité") appears in *Modern French Poets on Poetry*, ed. Robert Gibson (Cambridge: Cambridge University Press, 1979), 92n3. Eliot's claim that "genuine poetry can communicate before it is understood" can be found in his essay "Dante," in *Selected Essays of T. S. Eliot* (New York: Harcourt, Brace and World, 1950), 200. Wallace Stevens's begins his 1949 poem "Man Carrying Thing" with the lines "The poem must resist the intelligence/Almost successfully" (Collected Poems [New York: Vintage, 1982], 350). For Cavell's citing of Emerson ("nervous and wretched") and his own remarks about Walden's seeming to be "an enormously long and boring book," with "no suspense of plot," see his The Senses of Walden (San Francisco: North Point, 1981), 12, 20, 49. On the merging of description and significance, see Sharon Cameron, Writing Nature: Henry Thoreau's Journal (Chicago: University of Chicago Press, 1985), 5.

25. OPPORTUNITY

Thoreau's "I put the best face on the matter" is cited by Robert Sattelmeyer in "The Remaking of Walden," in the Walden, Civil Disobedience, and Other Writings, 3rd. ed., ed. William Rossi (New York: Norton, 2008), 501. Washington Irving's "Rip Van Winkle" is part of The Sketch Book of Geoffrey Crayon, Gent., in Washington Irving: History, Tales and Sketches (New York: Library of America, 1983); see esp. 770, 773, and 782. "Wakefield" is included in Hawthorne's Short Stories, ed. Newton Arvin (New York: Vintage, 1946). See 44 for the quotation beginning, "Amid the seeming confusion of our mysterious world." Thoreau's dictum, "Surely joy is the condition of life," appears in "Natural History of Massachusetts," in his Collected Essays and Poems (New York: Library of America, 2001), 22.

26. PHILOSOPHER

Nietzsche's remark is cited by J. P. Stern in A Study of Nietzsche (Cambridge: Cambridge University Press, 1979), 41. Wittgenstein's self-definition as "a business man" and his remark to Malcolm ("What is the use of studying philosophy") are both quoted in Ray Monk, Ludwig Wittgenstein: The Duty of Genius (New York: Penguin, 1990), 297, 424. Monk comments on Wittgenstein's appropriation of Freud's model of therapy, in How to Read Wittgenstein (New York: Norton, 2005), 73–74. "Suppose someone thinks he has found the solution to the 'problem of life'" appears in The Wittgenstein Reader, 2nd ed., ed. Anthony Kenny (Oxford, U.K.: Blackwell, 2006), 53. Wittgenstein's "We now demonstrate a method, by examples, and the series of examples can be broken off" also can be found in The Wittgenstein Reader, 59. The comment by Wittgenstein's students ("It was hard to see where all this often rather repetitive concrete detailed talk was leading to") is cited in D. A. T. Gasking and A. C. Jackson, "Wittgenstein as a Teacher," in Ludwig Wittgenstein: The Man and His Philosophy, ed. K. T. Fann (Atlantic Highlands, N.J.: Humanities Press, 1967), 51. Wittgenstein's remark that "it should be difficult to understand why I say it" is quoted by Severin Schroeder, Wittgenstein (Cambridge, U.K.: Polity, 2006), 26. Stanley Cavell, The Senses of Walden (San Francisco: North Point, 1981), 16, refers to *Walden*'s "drones of fact." Wittgenstein's "In order to see more clearly" comes from *Philosophical Investigations*, trans. G. E. M. Anscombe (Oxford, U.K.: Blackwell, 2001), 22e. Cavell's phrase "The problem is to establish his right to declare it [Thoreau's wisdom]" appears on 11 of *Senses*. For Richard J. Schneider's remark about Thoreau's neighbors' surprise at being called foolish, see his book *Henry David Thoreau* (New York: Twayne, 1987), 50. For Thoreau's letter to Harrison Blake, see Henry David Thoreau, *Letters to a Spiritual Seeker*, ed. Bradley P. Dean (New York: Norton, 2004), 36.

27. PROVING

For Robert Louis Stevenson's remark, see his essay "Henry David Thoreau," in his *Selected Essays* (Chicago: Regnery, 1959), 151. Lowell's observations about Thoreau's humorlessness and lack of spontaneity appear in his essay "Thoreau," reprinted in *Walden, Civil Disobedience, and Other Writings*, 3rd ed., ed. William Rossi (New York: Norton, 2008), 414, 412. Emerson's comment can be found in the same volume, 404–405. Leon Edel's judgment that "he was not a born writer" appears in his monograph *Henry D. Thoreau* (Minneapolis: University of Minnesota Press, 1970), 8.

For Barthes's distinction between labors of knowledge and writing, and for his definition of the "poetic" mode, see his autobiography, *Roland Barthes*, trans. Richard Howard (New York: Hill and Wang, 1977), 74, 152. Mallarmé's famous reply to Degas appears in *Modern French Poets on Poetry*, ed. Robert Gibson (Cambridge: Cambridge University Press, 1979), 150. Thoreau's assignment to his friend ("Let me suggest a theme for you") is quoted by Robert Louis Stevenson in "Henry David Thoreau," 149. The "unliterary" *Reports* is the subject of Thoreau's first major published essay, "Natural History of Massachusetts." Stanley Cavell observes that "impertinent" can refer to "the inquiries or the townsmen or the life" in *The Senses of Walden* (San Francisco: North Point, 1981), 46–47. Richard Poirier has noted the double meaning of *premises* in *A World Elsewhere: The Place of Style in American Literature* (Madison: University of Wisconsin Press, 1985), 86–87.

The quotations from the *Concord Freeman*'s account of Thoreau's fire come from Jeffrey S. Cramer, *Walden: A Fully Annotated Edition* (New Haven: Yale University Press, 2004), 91n80. Leon Edel argues that "less than a year before the retreat to Walden, Thoreau's reputation in Concord reached its lowest point." Thus, his adventure amounted to

a way of withdrawing from a town he experienced as hostile to him while at the same time remaining very close to it; a way also of asserting himself as an active "employed" man by embracing the career of writer and philosopher; an act of defiance which would demonstrate that his was a better way of life than that practiced by his fellows. Deeper still may have been the petulance of the child saying, in effect, to the town and to Emerson "see how homeless I am, you have forced me to live in a shanty away from all of you." He would arouse pity; he would also arouse interest. (*Henry D. Thoreau,* 21)

28. QUESTION

Sherman Paul, *The Shores of America: Thoreau's Inward Exploration* (Urbana: University of Illinois Press, 1972), 395, 184, 231. The leading discussion of Wittgenstein's philosophy as a kind of therapy appears in Gordon Baker, *Wittgenstein's Method: Neglected Aspects,* ed. Katherine Morris (Oxford, U.K.: Blackwell, 2006), esp. 146, 210; see also Morris's superb introduction to this volume, on which I have relied here, 1–18, esp. 6. Wittgenstein's comments—"The way I do philosophy," "like a piece of sugar in water," "let it drop," and "the old familiar words of the language are quite sufficient"—appear in *The Wittgenstein Reader,* 2ne ed., ed. Anthony Kenny (Oxford, U.K.: Blackwell, 2006), 54, 51. Their original source is Wittgenstein's *The Big Typescript.* The best discussion of Wittgenstein's philosophical anguish can be found in Ray Monk's classic biography, *Ludwig Wittgenstein: The Duty of Genius* ((New York: Penguin, 1990). Wittgenstein's suggestion that "the aspects of things that are most important for us are hidden" appears in *Philosophical Investigations,* trans. G. E. M. Anscombe (Oxford, U.K.: Blackwell, 2001), 43e. His remark that "the peculiarity of philosophical worry and its resolution might seem to be that it is like the anguish of an ascetic" is in *The Wittgenstein Reader,* 2nd ed., ed. Anthony Kenny (Oxford, U.K.: Blackwell, 2006), 53. Sharon Cameron's *Writing Nature: Henry Thoreau's Journal* (Chicago: University of Chicago Press, 1985), 109, 49, alerted me to three of the *Journal* entries I mention: "I omit the unusual ," "I begin to see . . . objects only when I leave off understanding them," and "The best thought is . . . without morality." Wittgenstein's remark about "loss of problems" appears in *Zettel,* ed. and trans. G. E. M. Anscombe (Berkeley: University of California Press, 1970), 82e. Thoreau's 1856 letter to Wiley is quoted in Joel Porte, *Emerson and Thoreau: Transcendentalists in Conflict* (Middletown: Wesleyan University Press, 1966), 112–13. Porte's book has greatly influenced this entry and others. Thoreau's essay "Walking" is included in *Walden, Civil Disobedience, and Other Writings,* 3rd. ed., ed. William Rossi (New York: Norton, 2008). "My desire for knowledge is intermittent" appears on 282–83. Wittgenstein's remarks about philosophy disappearing are in *Philosophical Investigations,* 44e.

29. READERS

Stanley Cavell says of Thoreau that "this writer is writing a sacred text" (*The Senses of Walden* [San Francisco: North Point, 1981], 14). For the passage from Thoreau's essay "Walking," see his *Collected Essays and Poems* (New York: Library of America, 2001), 226.

30. RENTS

André Bazin, *What Is Cinema?* 2 vols., trans. Hugh Gray (Berkeley: University of California Press, 1967–71), 2:13 ("For the first time an image of the world is formed automatically"), 14 ("decal or transfer," shroud of Turin, embalming), 163 (the veil of Veronica), 100 (Rossellini).

31. RUINS

Emerson's remark about *Robinson Crusoe* appears in Robert Louis Stevenson, "Henry David Thoreau," in Stevenson's *Selected Essays* (Chicago: Regnery, 1959), 150. Thoreau's "I never read a novel" is cited by Norman Foerster, "The Intellectual Heritage of Thoreau," in *Twentieth Century Interpretations of Walden,* ed. Richard Ruland (Englewood Cliffs, N.J.: Prentice-Hall, 1968), 48. The "Ktaadn" reference to *Crusoe* appears in *The Maine Woods* (New York: Library of America, 1985), 643. For Thoreau's other mentions of Crusoe, see *Walden,* ed. Jeffrey S. Kramer (New Haven: Yale University Press, 2004), 16n86. Cato's *De re rustica,* trans. Andrew Dalby, appears at www.soilandhealth.org/01aglibrary/010121cato/catofarmtext.htm. Emerson's comment about Thoreau's paradoxes appears in "Thoreau," reprinted in *Walden, Civil Disobedience, and Other Writings,* 3rd ed., ed. William Rossi (New York: Norton, 2008), 407.

32. SPIDER

Friedrich Nietzsche, *The Gay Science,* trans. Walter Kaufmann (New York: Vintage, 1974), 273–74. For Thoreau's remarks to Blake, see Henry David Thoreau, *Letters to a Spiritual Seeker,* ed. Bradley P. Dean (New York: Norton, 2004), 142. E. B. White, *Charlotte's Web* (New York: Harper and Row, 1952), 163–64. White's "Walden—1954" is reprinted in *Walden, Civil Disobedience, and Other Writings,* 3rd. ed., ed. William Rossi (New York: Norton, 2008); see esp. 443. Bill McKibben's remarks appear in his introduction to *Walden* (Boston: Beacon Press, 1997), xi.

33. STRIPPED

Emerson's remarks appear in "Thoreau," reprinted in *Walden, Civil Disobedience, and Other Writings,* 3rd. ed., ed. William Rossi (New York: Norton, 2008), 395–96. For Stevenson's comment, see his essay "Henry David Thoreau," in his *Selected Essays* (Chicago: Regnery, 1959), 133.

34. TRACKS AND PATHS

For Stephen Fender's valuable discussion of the railroad's effect on Concord, see his introduction to the Oxford World Classics edition of *Walden*

(Oxford: Oxford University Press, 1999), xvii–xix. Stanley Cavell pays particular attention to Thoreau's sense of how we describe our situation: see his *The Senses of Walden* (San Francisco: North Point, 1981). Wittgenstein's dictum, "The job to be done in philosophy," appears in *The Wittgenstein Reader*, 2nd ed., ed. Anthony Kenny (Oxford, U.K.: Blackwell, 2006), 46. For Sherman Paul's characterization of the Walden experiment as "domesticating oneself for inspiration," see his *The Shores of America: Thoreau's Inward Exploration* (Urbana: University of Illinois Press, 1972), 221. Nietzsche's comments on habits appear in *The Gay Science*, trans. Walter Kaufmann (New York: Vintage, 1974), 236–37.

35. UNEXPLORABLE

For the Ktaadn passage, see Thoreau, *A Week on the Concord and Merrimack Rivers, Walden; or, Life in the Woods, The Maine Woods, Cape Cod* (New York: Library of America, 1985), 640. For Adorno's remark, see *Aesthetics and Politics* (London: Verso, 1980), 129. On Thoreau's oscillation between the spiritual and scientific attitudes, see Sharon Cameron, *Writing Nature: Henry Thoreau's Journal* (Chicago: University of Chicago Press, 1985), 136–37. Susan Sontag's observation appears in *On Photography* (New York: Farrar, Straus and Giroux, 1977), 107: "Moralists who love photographs always hope that words will save the picture. (The opposite approach is that of the museum curator who, in order to turn a photojournalist's work into art, shows the photographs without their original captions)." Barthes's remark about "the unfolding of an image" appears in his *Roland Barthes*, trans. Richard Howard (New York: Hill and Wang, 1977), 152.

36. VOCATION

Emerson's "American Scholar" critique of recognized occupations can be found in his *Essays and Poems* (New York: Library of America, 1996), 54. In *The Shores of America: Thoreau's Inward Exploration* (Urbana: University of Illinois Press, 1972), Sherman Paul expands on this point:

> By rediscovering and affirming a spiritual life, by demanding something more than the prose existence of a materialistic life, Emerson had rejected the acknowledged vocations of his time. He had made them suspect, but had also, by leaving the new vocations free and undetermined, created difficulties for those who wished to follow him. (20)

For Thoreau's letter to Blake, see Henry David Thoreau, *Letters to a Spiritual Seeker*, ed. Bradley P. Dean (New York: Norton, 2004), 36. Emerson's characterization of Thoreau as "never idle or self-indulgent" appears in "Thoreau," reprinted in the *Walden, Civil Disobedience, and Other Writings*, 3rd. ed., ed. William Rossi (New York: Norton, 2008), 395. The passage from "Life

Without Principle" appears in *Thoreau: Collected Essays and Poems* (New York: Library of America, 2001), 351.

37. WITHOUT BOUNDS

William Drake provides a valuable discussion of how Thoreau's surveying influenced his concern with measurements in "*Walden,*" in *Thoreau: A Collection of Critical Essays,* ed. Sherman Paul (Englewood Cliffs, N.J.: Prentice-Hall, 1962), 83–84. Emerson's description of Thoreau as "a protestant" appears in his eulogy, "Thoreau," in *Walden, Civil Disobedience, and Other Writings,* 3rd ed., ed. William Rossi (New York: Norton, 2008), 395. I found Thoreau's "It is not easy to write in a journal what interests us" in Robert Richardson, *Henry Thoreau: A Live of the Mind* (Berkeley: University of California Press, 1986), 154. Andrew Delbanco's argument about Thoreau appears in his book *Required Reading: Why Our American Classics Matter Now* (New York: Farrar, Straus and Giroux, 1997), 39–40. Thoreau's letter in which he asks, "How shall we account for our pursuits if they are original?" is cited by Barbara Johnson, "A Hound, a Bay Horse, and a Turtle Dove: Obscurity in *Walden,*" in *Walden, Civil Disobedience, and Other Writings,* 484. For a superb discussion of Thoreau's remotivation of business terms, see Judith P. Saunders, "Economic Metaphor Redefined: The Transcendental Capitalist at Walden," in *Henry David Thoreau's "Walden,"* ed. Harold Bloom (New York: Chelsea House, 1987), 59–67.

Geoffrey O'Brien's remarks about Thoreau appear in his essay "Thoreau's Book of Life," *New York Review of Books,* 15 January 1987, 48 49. I discovered the crucial *Journal* entry, "I begin to see . . . objects only when I leave off understanding them," in Sharon Cameron, *Writing Nature: Henry Thoreau's Journal* (Chicago: University of Chicago Press, 1985), 49. Thoreau's delight in hearing the "purely wild and primitive American sound" of the Maine Indians appears in *A Week on the Concord and Merrimack Rivers, Walden; or, Life in the Woods, The Maine Woods, Cape Cod* (New York: Library of America, 1985), 696. Shelley's famous comment comparing "the mind in creation" to "a fading coal" appears in his "A Defence of Poetry," in his *Poetry and Prose,* ed. Donald H. Reiman and Neil Fraistat (New York: Norton, 2002), 531. For Barthes on Japan, see his book *The Empire of Signs,* trans. Richard Howard (New York: Hill and Wang, 1982), esp. 69–76. The biographer who referred to the *Week* as "a library of the shorter works of Henry Thoreau" is Henry Canby; his comment is cited in Sherman Paul, *The Shores of America: Thoreau's Inward Exploration* (Urbana: University of Illinois Press, 1972), 202. Wittgenstein's "If I am thinking about a topic" appears in his *Culture and Value,* trans. Peter Winch (Chicago: University of Chicago Press, 1980), 28e. David Pears makes boundaries central to Wittgenstein's philosophy: "In both his periods of philosophical activity his aim is to draw linguistic boundaries" (qtd. in Bryan Magee, *Modern British Philosophy* [New York: St. Martin's, 1971], 45). The phrase "the sense of the world must lie outside the world" appears in §6.41 of Wittgenstein's *Tractatus*. His "Lecture on Ethics" appears in *The Wittgenstein Reader*, 2nd ed., ed. Anthony Kenny (Oxford, U.K.: Blackwell, 2006), 258.

38. X MARKS WALDEN'S DEPTH

André Breton, *Nadja*, trans. Richard Howard (New York: Grove, 1960), 19–20.

39. YEARS

Robert Sattlelmeyer's comments appear in his superb essay "The Remaking of *Walden*," reprinted in *Walden, Civil Disobedience, and Other Writings*, 3rd. ed., ed. William Rossi (New York: Norton, 2008), 489–90. The seminal study of Thoreau's revisions remains J. Lyndon Shanley, *The Making of Walden* (Chicago: University of Chicago Press, 1957). In an essay on *The Prelude*, Susan Wolfson observes that "revision is not just compositional; it is the very trope of autobiography, a resistance . . . to arresting and fixing phantoms of conceit in a final frame of autobiographical argument." See Wolfson's "Revision as Form: Wordsworth's Drowned Man," in *William Wordsworth's The Prelude: A Casebook*, ed. Stephen Gill (Oxford: Oxford University Press, 2006), 78.

Continuity errors in fiction can not only break the realistic spell; they can also encourage train-spotting fans, as in the case of Sherlock Holmes. Wordsworth's famous remarks appear in the "Preface to *Lyrical Ballads*," in his *Selected Prose*, ed. John O. Hayden (New York: Penguin, 1988), 297 ("emotion recollected in tranquillity") and 283 ("our continued influxes of feeling"). Robert Frost's comment on *Walden*, originally appearing in the *Listener*, 26 August 1954, 319, is reprinted in *Twentieth Century Interpretations of Walden*, ed. Richard Ruland (Englewood Cliffs, N.J.: Prentice-Hall, 1968), 8. William E. Cain's remarks about Thoreau's apparent indifference to chronology appear in "Henry David Thoreau, 1817–1862: A Brief Biography," in *A Historical Guide to Henry David Thoreau* (Oxford: Oxford University Press, 2000), 42–43.

ANNOTATED BIBLIOGRAPHY

Thoreau and *Walden* have attracted an enormous secondary literature, much of it of unusually high quality. I have benefited greatly from it. I would like, however, to mention those books and essays that have contributed the most to this book. As Thoreau might have said, these have been *my* best teachers.

Buell, Lawrence. "Henry Thoreau Enters the American Canon." In *New Essays on Walden,* ed. Robert F. Sayre, 23–52. Cambridge: Cambridge University Press, 1992.

    A valuable essay tracing the reasons for Thoreau's growing reputation during the first half of the twentieth century.

Cain, William E. "Henry David Thoreau, 1817–1862: A Brief Biography." In *A Historical Guide to Henry David Thoreau,* ed. William E. Cain, 11–53. Oxford: Oxford University Press, 2000.

    Perhaps the best short account of Thoreau's life, and thus, an ideal starting point for someone coming to *Walden* for the first time.

Cameron, Sharon. *Writing Nature: Henry Thoreau's Journal.* Chicago: University of Chicago Press, 1985.

    This work argues that the *Journal,* both thematically and formally, represents Thoreau's vision more closely than his books, in which Thoreau made compromises to reach an audience.

Cavell, Stanley. *The Senses of Walden.* San Francisco: North Point, 1981.

    Cavell's book has been, since its original 1972 publication, the single most influential study of *Walden.*

Delbanco, Andrew. "Thoreau Faces Death." In Andrew Delbanco, *Required Reading: Why Our American Classics Matter Now,* 33–48. New York: Farrar, Straus and Giroux, 1997.

    A short essay that, like Geoffrey O'Brien's, raises original questions about Thoreau's relationship to language.

Edel, Leon. *Henry D. Thoreau*. Minneapolis: University of Minnesota Press, 1970.

    Edel doesn't seem to like Thoreau very much, but he uses his expertise in psychological biography to suggest aspects of Thoreau's personality unmentioned or underemphasized by other critics.

Emerson, Ralph Waldo. "Thoreau." In Henry David Thoreau, *Walden, Civil Disobedience and Other Writings*, ed. William Rossi, 394–409. New York: Norton, 2008.

    Emerson's eulogy, whose intermittent harshness Louisa May Alcott found inappropriate, remains one of the richest, most perceptive commentaries on Thoreau. It established the terms of Thoreau criticism for nearly a century.

Fender, Stephen. Introduction. In Henry David Thoreau, *Walden*, ix–xliii. Oxford: Oxford University Press, 1997.

    A remarkably rich essay, containing useful historical information. Fender's commentary on *Walden*'s snake passage (31–32) is especially acute.

Fink, Steven. "Thoreau and His Audience." In *The Cambridge Companion to Henry David Thoreau*, ed. Joel Myerson, 71–91. Cambridge: Cambridge University Press, 1995.

    A valuable essay on Thoreau's difficulty in finding a literary form commensurate with his abilities.

Krutch, Joseph Wood. *Henry David Thoreau*. New York: William Sloan, 1948.

    Published six years after F. O. Matthiessen's *American Renaissance*, with its chapter on *Walden*'s "organic form," Krutch's book furthered Thoreau's growing reputation as a central nineteenth-century author. A thorough account of Thoreau's life and writing, this study remains a useful introduction.

Milder, Robert. *Reimagining Thoreau*. Cambridge: Cambridge University Press, 1995.

    A recent work covering the *Week* and *Walden*, Milder's book is particularly good on the years after 1854.

O'Brien, Geoffrey. "Thoreau's Book of Life." *New York Review of Books*, 15 January 1987, 46–51.

    Perhaps the best short essay on Thoreau. Especially insightful regarding his vexed relationship with language.

Paul, Sherman. *The Shores of America: Thoreau's Inward Exploration*. Urbana: University of Illinois Press, 1958.

    Over fifty years after its first publication, this book remains the best single introduction to Thoreau, covering his life and works, from college themes to final essays. Paul's picture of Thoreau as a spiritual seeker, who experienced disappointment after the arcadia of Walden, may overstate Thoreau's subsequent melancholy. Nevertheless, anyone interested in Thoreau should read this book.

Peck, H. Daniel. "The Crosscurrents of *Walden*'s Pastoral." In *New Essays on Walden,* ed. Robert F. Sayre, 73–94. Cambridge: Cambridge University Press, 1992.

This essay has interesting things to say about Thoreau's decision to leave the pond.

Porte, Joel. *Emerson and Thoreau: Transcendentalists in Conflict.* Middletown: Wesleyan University Press, 1966.

Porte traces Thoreau's gradual, deliberate abandonment of transcendentalist Neoplatonism in favor of a Nietzschean embrace of the present.

Richardson, Robert D., Jr. *Henry Thoreau: A Life of the Mind.* Berkeley: University of California Press, 1986.

An intellectual biography that offers an ideal introduction to Thoreau.

Sattelmeyer, Robert. "The Remaking of *Walden.*" In Henry David Thoreau, *Walden, Civil Disobedience and Other Writings,* ed. William Rossi, 489–507. New York: Norton, 2008.

This essay's focus on the stages of *Walden*'s composition becomes the means for addressing Thoreau's conflicting, changing attitudes toward his work.

Saunders, Judith P. "Economic Metaphor Redefined: The Transcendentalist Capitalist at Walden." In *Henry David Thoreau's Walden,* ed. Harold Bloom, 59–67. New York: Chelsea House, 1987.

The best short introduction to Thoreau's cunning, punning use of business and economic terms for his own purposes.

Schneider, Richard. "*Walden.*" In *The Cambridge Companion to Henry David Thoreau,* ed. Joel Myerson, 92–106. Cambridge: Cambridge University Press, 1995.

Another ideal introduction to Thoreau, which discusses many issues crucial to *Walden.*

Shwartz, Ronald B. "Private Discourse in Thoreau's *Walden.*" In *Henry David Thoreau's Walden,* ed. Harold Bloom, 79–87. New York: Chelsea House, 1987.

This essay provocatively confronts the problem that *Walden* can prove intermittently boring.

Stevenson, Robert Louis. "Henry David Thoreau: His Character and Opinions." In Robert Louis Stevenson, *Selected Essays,* ed. George Scott-Moncrieff, 129–64. Chicago: Regnery , 1959.

Although rarely cited or anthologized, this 1880 essay, written less than twenty years after Thoreau's death, remains one of the best short pieces on *Walden*'s author. Stevenson finds Thoreau humorless and antisocial, but having struggled with his own vocational problems, he is especially acute on *Walden*'s economic thinking.

INDEX

The ABCs of Classic Hollywood
(Ray), 7
Adorno, Theodore, 138
Adventure, 9–10
Agassiz, Louis, 136
Alcott, Louisa May, 28
allusions, 122
ambivalence: assertion v. description, 17, 55–57, 72–73; austerity
v. sensuality, 63–65; cinematic
v. literary, 7, 53–54, 55–57, 72–74,
152–53; connotation v. denota-
tion, 55–57; contempt for work
v. tireless writing, 141–42; departure from Walden Pond, 84–86;
description v. moralizing, 51–52;
empirical v. transcendental,
15, 31–32; endeavor v. idleness,
66–74; experience v. experiment,
43, 122; experiment v. adventure,
9–10, 43, 44–45, 48, 55–57; expository v. poetic, 11–12, 55–57; ideas
v. words, 109–112; individualism
v. community, 39–42; internal
discovery v. external discovery,
46–47; literal v. figurative, 15;
living well v. professional ambition, 89–90; poetic v. expository,
11–12, 55–57; poetry v. science,
138–39; practice v. philosophy,
45–48, 55–57; purposefulness v.
passivity, 17–18; rearrangement
v. philosophy, 5, 91–93, 112–17,
157; rearrangement v. science, 15,
136; repetition of detail v. philosophical assertion, 106; resistance
to routine v. need for routine,
134–35; retreat from "real" world
v. living in it well, 105–107; science v. poetry, 138–39; simplicity
of life v. complexity of writing
style, 50, 115–17; sound v. written
language, 54, 121–22; toughness v.
fragility, 127; wakefulness v. sleep/
lethargy, 15–19. *See also* genre
issues; writing
American Dream, 78
"The American Scholar" (Emerson), 141
anti-conventional work stance,
141–42
anti-culture, 145
antihumanism, 137
Ants, 11–12
architecture, 49–50
aspect/"noticing an aspect," 28–30
assertion v. description, 17, 55–57,
72–73
austerity v. sensuality, 63–65
Awake, 13–19

Edel, Leon, 108
"The Eight Rules for Starting an
   Avant-Garde," 22–24
Eliot, T. S., 56, 96
Emerson, Ralph Waldo: contemporary success, 24; criticisms of
   Thoreau, 39; ecologist, 127–28; on
   reading Thoreau, 69; on Thoreau
   as writer, 108; Thoreau eulogy, 4,
   89–90; on Thoreau practicality,
   27; Thoreau relationship, 24–25;
   Thoreau vocational influence, 141;
   on Thoreau's "genius," 58; on Thoreau's "lack of ambition," 28; on
   Thoreau's paradoxes, 124; *Walden*
   omission, 108; on writing popular
   books, 123
empirical v. transcendental, 15, 31–32
endeavor v. idleness, 66–74
environmental movement of today,
   127–28
eternal recurrence, 125–27
"The Evolution of the Language of
   Cinema" (Bazin), 72–73
existentialism, 29, 89
experience v. experiment, 43, 122
Experiment, 43–48
experiment v. adventure, 9–10, 43,
   44–45, 48, 55–57
exploitation of opportunity, 150–51
expository v. poetic, 11–12, 55–57

Fashion, 49–52
Fender, Stephen, 13–14, 47
filmmaking process, 152–53. *See also*
   cinematic v. literary
Fitchburg train, 54, 132
Fitzgerald, F. Scott, 74–75
Flaubert, Gustave, 145
Flute, 53–57
French impressionist painters, 21–24
Freud, Sigmund, 104
Friedman, Thomas, 137
frontiers, 75–76
Frost, Robert, 153

Fuller, Margaret, 82, 108
frustrations of reader, 4, 96–99,
   118–20. *See also* ambivalence;
   genre issues; redefinition of
   words; repetition; writing

The Gay Science (Nietzsche),
   125–26, 134
Genius, 58–60
genre issue, 9
genre issues: departure from and
   return to "real world," 100–103;
   instruction manual, 50; literary genre stripped of literary
   characteristics, 129–31; practical environmentalist's volume,
   128; sacred text interpretation
   and impracticality, 120; self-help
   book, 46, 47; sermon, 118–20;
   training manual, 102–103; travel/
   adventure book, 46–47; unavail-
   ability of genre fitting Thoreau
   genius, 58–59
George Bailey, 101
goals, 45, 102
Good and Evil, 61–62
The Great Gatsby (Fitzgerald),
   74–75

habit, 134–35. *See also* track and
   path metaphors
Hawthorne, Nathaniel, 39, 101
Heidegger, Martin, 86–87
Higher Laws, 63–65
Hoar, Edward, 111

ideas v. words, 109–112
Idleness, 66–74
impressionist painters, 21–24
inconsistencies. *See* ambivalence
individualism v. community, 39–42
internal discovery v. external discovery, 46–47
Irving, Washington, 101
It's a Wonderful Life (movie), 101

James, Henry, 39, 58
James, Henry, Sr., 108
Johnson, Samuel, 60
the *Journal* (Thoreau): composition method and writing plan, 5, 81, 86; description v. narration, 69–70, 137, 139; moralizing v. description, 51–52; relative freedom of form, 146–47; sensuousness in simplicity, 68–69; Walden Pond sojourn purpose, 86
July 1845, 75–78

Kittlybenders, 79–83
Krutch, Joseph Wood, 7
Ktaadn, 67, 123, 137–38, 142

language: ambiguity of word meaning, 110–12; business and economic terminology, 144–45; creative personal usage, 145–46; as game, 94, 144–45; perceived inadequacy, 145–46; redefinition of everyday words, 67–69, 97–99; resistance to rules of language, 144–45; as trap or pitfall, 144–45
Lapine, James, 142
Leaving Walden, 84–87
"liberating word," 30
"Life Without Principle" (Thoreau), 142
literal v. figurative, 15
"Literary Ethics" (Emerson), 89–90
living well v. professional ambition, 89–90
Loos, Adolf, 50–51
Lowell, James Russell, 39
Lyrical Ballads (Wordsworth), 136

The Maine Woods (Thoreau), 67, 81, 137–38, 142
Mallarmé, Stéphane, 96, 109
mapping, 149–51
McKibben, Bill, 128
measurement, 149–51

method: compared to Breton's, 151; as involving meticulous description, 93, 97, 106, 115; as less doctrine than practice, 105; Thoreau's v. Wittgenstein's, 92–93, 106, 115, 147–48; Thoreau's writing method, 5, 81–83, 110, 145–47, 152–55; "tuning in" with the world, 87; "wakefulness" or alertness achievement, 16; of the Walden "experiment," 44–45, 101–102; of writing about Walden, 5–8
Molting, 88–90
molting metaphor, 87–88
moods, 87–88
Morris, Katherine, 114–15
Moseley, Catherine, 53–54
music, 53–54
mysteriousness, 11

Nadja (Breton), 48, 150
Name, 91–94
"Natural History of Massachusetts" (Thoreau), 114
Nature (Emerson), importance to Thoreau, 26, 28
nature v. words, 109–112
Nausea (Sartre), 10
New Yorker, 127–28
Nietzsche, Friedrich: on approaching deep problems, 82–83; common man v. authentic individual, 41–42; depth metaphor, 82–83; eternal recurrence, 125–26; fragmentation, 147; on habits, 134; on philanthropy, 77–78; on philosophy as way of living, 104; on reading discontinuous works, 7–8; rhetoric and notoriety, 61; surveying role, 125–26
"Notes toward a Supreme Fiction" (Stevens), 18
Numbers, 95

O'Brien, Geoffrey, 34, 37, 48, 145–46

fragmentation, 5; frontier metaphor, 75; goals, 86–87, 102; history, 2; hybrid nature, 56, 60; as instruction manual, 50; intensity of opening chapters, 34–35; lack of narrative, 59–60; as mosaic, 82; Nature as redefiner of information, 10; organizing modes, 11–12; as proof rather than experiment, 48; prose style, 50; purpose, 86–87; reason for writing, 3–4; as recording of a process, 153–55; redefinition of information, 10; as self-help book, 47, 48; soundtrack, 53, 54; as sum of multiple histories simultaneously present, 152; as training manual for writing life, 57, 102–103; as travel/adventure book, 46–47; writing, 81, 142; writing methodology, 5; writing time frame, 152

Walden Pond: departure, 84–87; goals of experience, 67, 102; as ideal permanence symbol, 31–32; location, 2, 11; proximity to home and civilization, 36–38; reality metaphor, 79–80; as setting for life-and-death struggle, 33–35

A Week on the Concord and Merrimack Rivers (Thoreau), 142; commercial failure, 20–21, 100; descriptive passages, 113; drummer imagery, 40–41; moralizing v. description, 51–52; non-narrative nature, 59–60; original purpose, 2, 34; writing, 67, 81, 142

"What Novels Can Do That Films Can't" (Chatman), 55–56

White, E. B., 127

wildness, 136

Wiley, B. B., 51

Without Bounds, 144–48

Wittgenstein, Ludwig: as anticipated by Thoreau, 3; on arcane language v. old and familiar, 115; on colors, 31, 32; on constraints of ordered writing forms, 147; on disappearance of philosophical questions, 117; language game, 93–94; movie preferences, 53; on perception change, 28–29; on philosophy, 8, 104, 106, 114–15, 132; on rearrangement, 92–93; repudiation of ornament, 51; search for key to perception change, 29; Thoreau commonality, 7; on writing philosophy, 30

Wolfe, Tom, 23

words. *See* language

Wordsworth, William, 16–17, 23–24, 44, 122, 136–37

work, 45–46, 141–43

worth, 156–57

writing: accomplished at Walden Pond, 67, 79–80; "Civil Disobedience" (Thoreau), 81; complexity of prose style, 115–17; fresh starts v. heroic book foundation, 123–24; as means of engaging with the world, 146; as method of experiencing, 122; narrative absence, 11–12, 59–60; Thoreau attitude, 10; written language v. sound, 121–22. *See also* cinematic v. literary

writing for a living, 21–27, 45–46, 100

X Marks Walden's Depth, 149–51

Years, 152–55

Zanzibar, 156–57

ROBERT B. RAY is Professor of English at the University of Florida, where he has also served as director of film studies. His previous books include *A Certain Tendency of the Hollywood Cinema, 1930–1980; The Avant-Garde Finds Andy Hardy; How a Film Theory Got Lost* (IUP 2001); and *The ABCs of Classic Hollywood*. He has been a member of the Vulgar Boatmen, who have released four records, including *You and Your Sister* and *Wide Awake*.